English doesn't SUCK:
IT ROCKS!

English doesn't SUCK:

IT ROCKS!

By

Alice Courtney, Bobbi Creighton, and Sue Skidmore

Cover design by

Kolby McLean and Will Zandler

Dedication

To Ashley, Dave, Denice, Kolby, J., J., and the M&Ms

In memory of Hiawatha and Stan

English Doesn't Suck: It Rocks! is published by DABROADS 3, LLC, Phoenix, Arizona, 2010. All Rights Reserved. No part of this book may be reproduced in any manner without expressed, written permission of DABROADS3. For information, please correspond through *englishdoesntsuck.com*.

First Edition

ISBN 978-1-453-84095-5

Table of Contents

Introduction	*ix*
We Get It	*xiii*
Absolute Truths	*xv*
The Big Eight	**1**
Nouns	3
Pronouns	3
Verbs	4
Adjectives	5
Adverbs	6
Prepositions	6
Conjunctions	7
Interjections	8
Mark It!	**11**
Punctuation:	
End marks	13
Those less famous	14
The Seven Deadly Sins of Writing	**25**
Laziness: Writing Hideous Sentences	27
Anger: Composing Disagreeable Sentences	29
Greed: Splitting Hares, Not Infinitives	32
Lust: Dangling Your Participle or Misplacing Your Modifier	33
Envy: Coveting Unbalanced Sentences	34
Gluttony: Elimating Obesity in Writing	35
Pride: Being a Doofus	36

PWR	45
Prewriting	47
Writing	49
Writing Breeds:	50
Paragraph	51
Business communications	53
Essay	57
Narrative Paper	62
Argumentation/Persuasion Paper	66
Compare and Contrast Paper	70
Cause and Effect Paper	73
Process Paper	78
Descriptive Paper	84
Research paper	89
Revising Strategies	98
Things that are Just Sick and Wrong	**101**
Parent Advice	**109**
Suggested Topics	116
Prescription Practice	**121**
Acknowledgements	**135**
Appendix	**137**
Paragraph outline	139
Essay Outline	140
Index	**143**

"Put your hands together and give it up for my band, Phleby and the Sucker Pluckers!"

Introduction

There's no such thing as gravity; the whole world sucks!

Well, not quite. These things suck:

- Losing your cell phone
- Vacuum cleaners
- Broken fingernails and broken hearts
- Split ends
- Vampires
- Leeches
- Homework
- Standardized tests
- Straws
- Standing in line at the movie theater
- Anything that disrupts internet service, sleep, or video games
- Being grounded

Even our icon, Phleby, a pesky mosquito sucks. Named Cassandra at birth, she dreamed of becoming a renowned, rock star. However, her mother and grandmother had other plans; they assumed she would inherit the family-owned, blood-sucking laboratory near Cate Mercy Hospital. When Cassandra morphed into an insect, she flew to Seattle, changed her name to Phleby, and joined a garage band. After a year, she was writing songs, playing lead guitar, and singing. She soon grew bored of the band, decided to develop a solo act, and hire a mega-agent to book super-star gigs. At her first, solo performance, she opened with her original song, "You Make Me Want to Itch." Phleby became an overnight sensation! Radio stations were flooded with requests to play "You Make Me Want to Itch," and her album, by the same title, went platinum in six weeks. She appeared on talk shows, internet sites, and billboards. Her clothing, perfume, and jewelry lines became the cornerstone of every major department store from Maine to California. Then several weeks ago, she was chosen as "Top Rock Artist of the Year." When Madame Duh Duh presented the award, Phleby sucked up her emotion and said, "I'd like to thank my producer, my sound mixer, my agent, my parents, and my fans for making this possible. Please know, though, that I would not be here today without Mrs. Baridingles, my English teacher. She taught me how to write, and so Mrs. Baridingles, this is for you."

We were so overcome by Phleby's acknowledgement of the power of English teachers, we contacted her agent. Graciously, Phleby agreed to help us, help you.

Crank up the volume, and read on!

We Get It

Any person learning English will find it overwhelming. Imagine trying to decipher these sentences:

1. The psychologist had to subject the subject to a series of tests.
2. When I saw the tear in my dress, I shed a tear.
3. The Marine made a decision to desert his dessert in the desert.
4. A dove dove into the underbrush.
5. The clothes were hung too close to the closet door, and I couldn't close it.
6. After he had read a book about the red tide, he stated, "It was a good read."
7. My invalid mother discovered her health insurance was invalid.
8. The buck does numerous antics when he sees a herd of does.
9. The gardener loved to produce produce.
10. The musician painted a bass on his bass horn.
11. At the present time, there is no one available to present the present to the winner.
12. As he was led from the cell, the prisoner was asked to lead the way to the spot where he had buried the lead pipe.
13. It was difficult to wind the kite string in the high wind.
14. He did object when he learned he was no longer the object of her affection.

If that isn't enough, consider this pronunciation nightmare.

Though we were thorough in our investigation, it was rough to determine if we were through. We thought we provided tough evidence, and our client decided there was no more dough to warrant further research. So until the proverbial bough breaks, we ought not worry. We will remain on the payroll of the public trough.

English is NOT easy, but don't worry, Phleby is here to suck the misery out of English. With her help and our guidance, you can do it.

BUT I HATE ENGLISH, IT SUC....

Excuse us! Don't finish the sentence! We really **do get it.** We understand that you:

- Want to vomit when asked to submit something in writing
- Panic when having to send a memo to your teacher, professor, or important adult
- Cheat your way through English classes by downloading papers from the internet (Hope you weren't stupid enough to copy your older sister's term paper and submit it as yours. Did you forget? She had your teacher, Mr. Red Disbfour.)
- Live in fear that you'll be "outed" as an incompetent writer

We are here to save you from embarrassment! Our humorous reference guide can save your sorry, hind end, make your parents proud of your accomplishments, and build your confidence. We double, double dare you to turn the page.

Absolute Truths

Consider this as a one-time, limited-offer, bonus gift! Our former partner, Dr. Mallorcus, gave us this information right before she went bonkers from teaching English to ninth graders. After much discussion, we have added this section for your entertainment and enjoyment at **no** additional cost. Read on.

Miss U.R. Baridingles
513 Glacier Road
Wheeler, North Carolina
October 21, 2011

Dr. Dorcas Mallorcus
8519 E. Bumble Lee Trail
Earwax, California 63541

Dear Dorcas:

Of course, I remember you. You were one of my promising students forty years ago, even though you talked too much when you should have been listening to the my presentation. I recently retired from Sag Hollow School District after a fifty-one-year career as a middle and a high school English teacher. I feel honored that you would ask my advice about your book, *English Isn't Rocket Science.* One thing comes to mind about my long tenure; the play doesn't change--just the actors. Students today have far more access to the world. True, they have piercings, tattoos, and pink hair, unlike your generation. However, they have amazing technology to discover anything they want to know. They can download a book in less than thirty seconds, take a guided tour of a Paris museum without ever leaving their desks, and visually and orally chat with children in Beijing.

Thus, Dorcas, let me offer you this advice. Add an additional section to your book. Title it: **Absolute Truths.** Absolute Truths are like the play, they never change. They are undeniable comments about life that have withstood the test of time. For example, your book title is an **Absolute Truth:** *English Is NOT Rocket Science.* Throughout your book, scatter these absolute truths in an entertaining way.

Thank you, Dorcas, for your letter. Best of luck to you.

Sincerely,

U.R. Baridingles

Okay? Do you get it? Absolute truths will be found throughout our book. Memorize them, so you can vomit them back to your children and grandchildren. Don't give us attitude, that you will **never** do that. You will; trust us. Absolute truths will be **bolded**, asterisked, and noted as *(AT). Behold the following examples:
- **Liposuction sucks. *(AT)**
- **The world is bigger than the 8th grade. *(AT)**
- **You *do* have something to wear. *(AT)**
- **Chewing fingernails as a dietary supplement is bogus. *(AT)**

"You need these to write the songs I sing."

The Big 8

The Big Eight!

Judging by the size of most grammar books, you have been fooled into thinking that there are hundreds, if not thousands, of parts of speech. This is a well-known conspiracy between professors and publishers. There are only eight, and your writing will suck if you don't use them correctly!

1. **Noun**: the name of a thing (You have heard it as the name of a person, place or thing; we just abbreviated it.)

   - It was 6 AM, and the **alarm** went off way too early this **morning**. — nouns
   - Having just returned from **Los Angeles, Roxy** felt as though she had just gone to **bed** an **hour** or so ago.
   - Oh well, **feet** on the **floor**; it was **time** to get **things** rolling.

2. **Pronoun:** replaces the name of a *thing*

These are divided into five types.

   Subject: replaces the "who" or the "what" of the sentence

| I | you | he | she | it | we | they |

   - **She** headed for the shower.
   - OMG! **It** was nothing but cold water!

   Object: gets the brunt of the action from the who of the sentence

| me | you | him | her | it | us | them |

   - As the cold water shocked **her** back to reality, Roxy discovered she had stopped thinking about **them**.
   - She had seen numerous Hollywood stars during her vacation and had wondered, "Are they truly just like **us**?"

- She was going to make **it** a day to remember, no matter what.

Possessive: These show ownership of something.

| mine | your(s) | his | hers | its | our(s) | their(s) |

- She made it to the breakfast table and discovered **her** eggs were stone cold and **her** orange juice lukewarm.
- Further, a fly was gasping **its** last breath as it drowned in someone's leftover cereal.

Demonstrative: Think of Vanna White pointing at the big letters; it's a demonstration.

| this | that | these | those |

- **This** was going to be a great day despite **that** shower issue and **that** dead fly.
- Roxy would put aside **these** irritations and focus on what lay ahead.

Interrogative: used to ask questions

| what | which | who | whose | whom |

- **What** would be waiting around the next corner for her?
- **Which** way could her day go but up?

3. **Verb:** what *things* do

- Roxy **walked** into the garage and **got** in her late grandmother's old sedan.
- Anticipating the roar of the engine, she **was disgusted** with the familiar clicking of a dead battery. (Dead batteries really suck on manic Mondays! Of course, dead batteries also suck Tuesdays through Fridays.)
- Aaron, her stupid freshman brother, **smiled** a tinsel-toothed grin as they **headed** for the bus stop.

- **Imagine** the horror of being seventeen and of having to ride on the same bus as your brother!

 *You Suck Uh-Oh!*

NOUN (or pronoun) + Verb = Sentence

It's a miracle if you think about it. If you do not have those basic parts, you have committed a catastrophic mistake from here on referred to as a *You Suck Uh-Oh!*

The rest of the *Big 8* add the color, emphasis, and interest to your writing. These help you *show* your reader instead of *tell* him. Using these means you've grown up and put on your 'big girl' panties!

4. Adjectives: describe *things*

- The **crowded** bus was similar to a locker room; the **overpowering** smell of **cheap** hairspray and AXE® hit hard as the **bi-fold** door swung open.
- The **noise** level was almost as **loud** and **obnoxious** as the alarm had been earlier.

Adjectives in comparison:

- Add **-er** when comparing two things: The boy greeting Roxy at the front of the bus was **hot**, but the one sitting a few rows back was **hotter**.

- Add **-est** when comparing three or more things: Of all the guys on the bus, the one in the back row was the **hottest**. With most adjectives that have two or more syllables, do not change the form of the adjective. Instead, use the word **more** when comparing two things and **most** when comparing three or more things:

- Sitting with any of these guys would be **more enjoyable** than sitting with Aaron, but getting to the back of the bus would be **most enjoyable**.

- **NEVER use both an –er and more, or both an –est and most.**

Incorrect example: *When she moved toward the back of the bus, she was convinced that this might be the **most happiest** day of her life.*

Correct Example: *When she moved toward the back of the bus, she was convinced that this might be the **happiest** day of her life.*

5. Adverbs: describe how, when, where, and how much. Most, but not all, adverbs end in **-ly**.

- The bus **suddenly** jerked to a start; Roxy ducked **clumsily** and plopped into the nearest seat, smacking the guy beside her with her backpack **really** hard.
- She **carefully** looked up to find she was sitting next to BJ Monroe, the terror of Creighton High School.
- Aaron **excitedly** smiled his tinsel-toothed grin **even** bigger, as Roxy tried to apologize **quickly** to BJ.

6. Prepositions: words that tell anywhere a mosquito goes, i.e. **in** your ear, **between** your toes, **after** dark, but never **at** the end **of** a sentence!

Behold the list of common prepositions.

above	about	across	along	among
around	at	before	behind	below

beside	between	by	down	during
except	for	from	in	inside
into	of	off	on	onto
past	through	to	toward	under
up	upon	with	within	without

This isn't the entire list, just some of the most common. The full list numbers well over 50.

- **Around** the corner, the bus jumped a curb, and Roxy almost flew **into** the seat **across** the aisle.
- **Without** hesitation, BJ grabbed Roxy's waist and safely tossed her **onto** his lap.
- Then she noticed that BJ had a tattoo that ran **from** his wrist **to** his forearm.
- She never knew anyone **with** a tattoo!
- Thinking she'd like to ask him **about** it, she was embarrassed. After all, she was sitting **around** all the kids she knew **from** school. Plus, BJ was the well-known "bad-boy" **at** Creighton.

7. **Conjunctions:** It is easiest to remember these as **FANBOYS:** *For, And, Nor, But, Or, Yet, So.* These link words, ideas, and sentences.

    - As the bus slowed to a stop in front of the school, Roxy knew she had to ask, **or** she would not have another opportunity.
    - "BJ, I am curious about your tattoo, **and** I need to understand why you chose it."
    - "**Either** tell me your name, **or** I won't answer your stupid question, doll," he replied.
    - "Roxy."
    - "Well, foxy Roxy, my mom always told me that

vacuum cleaners suck, **so** I chose this tattoo: **English DOESN'T SUCK.** I'm going to college next fall to study screen-play writing, **for** I hope to win an Academy Award.®

- Never think that bad boys are dumb, **nor** underestimate their dreams.

- Six years later, BJ **and** I attended the Academy presentation in Los Angeles, **and** BJ won!

Either/or go together as do *neither, nor, never,* and *not.*

8. Interjections: Expressions of strong feeling or surprise, such as ***whoopee, whoa, ouch, oh, hey***

Often an interjection is a fragment, like **Duh!,** that is followed by an exclamation point. While we would love to give you a complete list, we have discovered that interjections are a little like having ADHD, they come and go pretty quickly. Below, please find our best lists of interjections and the sentences they inhabit.

Old School Interjections

Alas	Alack	Cool	Egad	Eek
Eureka	Gadzooks	Golly Gee	Neato	Shazam

Common Interjections

Ah	Aha	Bravo	Cool	Darn
Hey	Oh	Ouch	Whoa	Wow

Current Interjections

Arrgh	As if	Bitchin'	Cool	Duh
Fosho	Gotcha	Hello	Holy…	Not
OMG	Sick	Tru dat	Uh oh	WTF

Do you like to interrupt or be the center of attention in a conversation? Then use an interjection.

- **OMG!** BJ won!
- **Hey!** Are you still my brother, Aaron?
- **Arrgh**! I'm getting a headache!

"Don't Save Your Commas for Your Momma" is my new album!

Mark It!

Mark It!

Punctuation signs are used to clarify meaning. Read the following:

Shes a self described computer butt nugget who would rather be surfing the Maui waves she hates to be alone with a computer its a nightmare

This is rat dung! Is Shes a name? Or did the writer mean She's (she is)? Does Shes like or hate waves? We will never know.

End Marks: those marks placed at the butt end of your miraculous sentence!

1. Period (.): a dot at the end of a sentence, not a monthly concern.
- My brother cheats at Dominoes.
- When I leave the room to get a soda, he overturns all of the tile and positions them where he can find them.
- On his turn to draw, he miraculously picks up the best tile.
- Little does he know that I secretly video-taped his cheating spree.
- He can no longer deny that he is a loser.

2. Exclamation point (!): after a word or a group of words that show surprise.
- You spray-painted the dog!
- Max can't be purple!
- Mom is going to kill you!

3. Question mark (?): at the end of a question.
- Why didn't you turn in your math homework?

- Wasn't it in your backpack?
- Did you leave it in the car?
- Did you give it to Julie to copy?

Other less-famous marks that can be used anywhere.

4. Comma (,): Most have heard or read about the Canadian company that almost lost over two million dollars by omitting a comma that was vital to contractual language. Others may recall an elementary school lesson about missing commas, as in the following:

"Let's eat Tommy." Now, unless this was spoken by Alfred Packer, we suspect the writer meant: *"Let's eat, Tommy."*

There are SIX major uses of a comma.

A. Words in a series: Think of a grocery list or a 'To Do' list; then, instead of making the list, put them side by side with commas to separate the items.
- Momma is going to the grocery store for water, lettuce, cereal, water, toilet paper, coffee, bread, milk, wine, water, and chicken. Momma is an aguaholic.
- I saw London, I saw France, and I saw Collette's underpants.

Think of a number of adjectives that can be used to describe this actual event that occurred in Phoenix, AZ in July.

Here is our attempt:

- On a steaming, sultry, July day, Miss Calamity Bean opened the black, iron gate. While her checkered, weathered, fly mask prevented her from estimating the depth of the water, she wandered into the clear, cool, water. When her shoeless, frantic, hysterical, owner called 911....

- Josh bought three t-shirts, a pair of designer jeans, a graphing calculator, and a high-tech cell phone; he was ready for the first day of school.

- On Monday, Josh used his cell phone to download his class schedule, to buy an activity pass, and to order a yearbook.

B. Interrupters: Place a comma *before and after* words that interrupt the flow of a sentence, not to be confused with lava.

- Mr. Arnholt, **principal of Shea High School**, retired before he could be fired.
- I, **of course,** am a diva because I'm the youngest.

C. FANBOYS (*For, And, Nor, But, Or, Yet, So)*: Place a comma between two complete thoughts connected with a FANBOYS.

- Sissy began playing golf when she was four, **but** she never qualified for a position on the high school varsity team.
- Sissy had a great swing, **yet** she always clutched and missed every putt.

D. Introductory Material: Place a comma after the opening intro.

- **On behalf of the producers of *Horror on Main Avenue,*** I regret to inform you that you have not been chosen for the part of Crazy Charlie.
- **Checking in both directions for oncoming traffic,** Jake jogged across the intersection.

E. Everyday Stuff that needs to be separated: Place a comma between names and titles, dates, addresses, and numbers.

- **Title**: Bobbi Creighton, **PhD,** is the principal author of *English Doesn't SUCK: It Rocks.*
- **Dates**: On March 3, 2010, the first edition of *English Doesn't SUCK: It Rocks* was published.
- **Address**: The corporate offices of *English Doesn't SUCK: It Rocks* are at 513 Elm Street, Commaville, Arkansas.
- **Numbers:** What are the chances *English Doesn't SUCK: It Rocks* will become a best seller: 1 in 1,000,000,000,000,000,000,000?

F. Direct Quotations: Use a comma and quotation marks to set off direct quotes.

- Mark Twain once said, "When a teacher calls a boy by his entire name, it means trouble."
- "I never expected to see the day," mused Will Rogers, "when girls get sunburned in the places they do."

5. Apostrophe ('): This is a comma under the influence. Yes, it's high.

Use an apostrophe:

A. To show possession or ownership--singular words

- The boy's stinky socks littered the locker room floor. (the socks belonging to the boy)
- Shea High School's locker rooms reek of stinky socks. (the locker rooms belonging to Shea High school)
- Jaimie, Luis, and Hank's coach yelled at the boys to pick up their stinky socks. (the coach of Jaimie, Luis, and Hank--NOTE the apostrophe is placed on the last word in the group, not the others. If the three boys had **different** coaches, it would be expressed: Jaimie's, Luis's, and Hank's coaches yelled at the boys to pick up their stinky socks.)
- *For singular words ending in s:* The school bus's emergency exit was blocked with stinky socks and sneakers.

B. To show possession or ownership--plural words. The apostrophe follows *after* the s.

- The boys' stinky socks littered the locker room floor. (the socks belonging to the boys on the team)

- Most of the Arizona high schools' graduates went to college.
- **Teenagers' lives thrive on drama and their parents' credit cards. *(AT)**

C. To show contractions--the apostrophe replaces a missing letter or letters

I	+	am	=	I'm
You	+	are	=	You're
He/She	+	is	=	He's/She's
I	+	will	=	I'll
You	+	will	=	You'll
He/She	+	will	=	He'll/She'll
I	+	would/had	=	I'd
You	+	would/had	=	You'd
He/She	+	would/had	=	He'd/She's
We	+	are	=	We're
They	+	are	=	They're
We	+	will	=	We'll
They	+	will	=	They'll
We	+	would/had	=	We'd
They	+	would/had	=	They'd
Let	+	us	=	Let's
Who	+	is/has	=	Who's

D. The vanishing not

Can	+	not	=	Can't
Should	+	not	=	Shouldn't
Could	+	not	=	Couldn't
Would	+	not	=	Wouldn't
Do	+	not	=	Don't
Does	+	not	=	Doesn't
Will	+	not	=	Won't
Was	+	not	=	Wasn't
Were	+	not	=	Weren't

You Suck Uh-Oh!

It (the neutered pronoun) Use an apostrophe if your intent is: it is or it has.

It's been an awesome experience being in the bio-medical class at the hospital.

  DO NOT use an apostrophe if the word 'it' possesses something.

*The cat licked **its** paws.*

Read your sentence out loud and substitute *it is* where you're thinking of putting *it's*. Nine times out of ten, you will hear it and make the right choice! Other confusing contractions:

- Your and you're

Your = belonging to you

You're = You are

If **you're** going to the dance on Saturday night, **your** ticket must be purchased by Thursday.

- Whose and who's

Whose = belonging to whom

Who's = who is

Who's going to the dance? **Whose** parents are available to drive?

- They're = they are

Ashley and Jason have a date to the dance, and **they're** going to take a limo.
- Their = belong to them

Their parents are paying for **their** styling ride.
- There = not here

Look! The purple limo is parked over **there**.

6. **Colon (:):** two vertical dots on top of each other.

There are four major uses of the colon:

A. **Set off a formal list of items**
   - Before going on the mall, please complete the following chores: finish your homework, mow the lawn, feed the dogs, and clean your pig sty.
   - Teachers often grade papers focusing on these: content, ideas, organization, voice, spelling and punctuation.

B. **Introduction of a formal business letter**
   - Dear Sir:
   - To whom it may concern:
   - Hey Stupid:

C. Time
- When we were in middle school, we all dropped our pens on the floor at 10:15 AM.
- The substitute teacher cried and yelled at us until the period ended at 10:42 AM.
- You came in at what time? It was more like 11:30 PM. You're grounded!

D. Anatomy 101
- See your doctor for correct usage.

7. Semicolon (;): (half a colon) a comma with a dot on top of it. We like to refer to it as a **big-boy** comma.

A semicolon is used to separate two, complete sentences. This punctuation mark is used in place of comma + a FANBOYS.
- School was dismissed early; Tom sat bored at his computer.
- He wanted to do something; he remembered he had no money.
- He's spent it all last week on a stupid date with a stupid girl; he was stupid.

8. Quotation Marks (" "): Quotation marks are two pair of ditzy commas, flying high across the page. While some tweens adore using quotation marks to emphasize words, it is sick and wrong.

Use quotation marks to:

A. Signal a direct quotation
- "Where did you get your hair cut?" asked Wendy.
- "On my head," he answered.
- According to James Wilber, "The first hundred years are the worst." Then he added, "Once you reach 100; everything is downhill."

B. Quote no more than four lines of poetry or prose (For a research paper, consult style requirements.)
- "Out damn'd spot! Out, I say!" was spoken by Lady Macbeth, and she wasn't talking about ring around the collar.
- In her famous poem, she wrote, "Hickory, Dickory, Dock/ Two mice ran up the clock. The clock struck one/ and the other dropped dead of fright."

C. Quote within a quote (This is tricky.) Single quotation marks are used to enclose a quotation **within** a quotation.
- The graduation speaker said, "One of the most powerful advertising slogans is 'Just Do It®!' So I challenge you graduating seniors to go out there and do it!"
(The speaker is quoting an advertising slogan)
- "'It's better to keep your mouth shut and appear stupid than to open it and remove all doubt' according to Mark Twain, and I should remember that before I express an opinion on something I no absolutely nothing about--like fixing my laptop," whined Susan. (Susan is quoting Mark Twain.)

Indirect quotations, or those that do not use exact words, require NO quotation marks as in the following:

- Bruce swore he did not eat the last blue raspberry popsicle, yet his tongue and lips were blue.
- When asked why he denied eating the popsicle, Bruce replied that he thought he could get away with it. After all, he'd hidden the wrapper and the stick under his mattress.

9. Hyphen (-): This little, punctuation mark is so odd that we suggest you consult a dictionary because some words require hyphens, such as mother-in-law, while others like bridegroom do not. His **brother-in-law** posted a picture of the **textbook** on his **homepage.**

There are four uses of a hyphen:

A. Compound adjectives that describe a thing (noun)

- My **six-year-old** brother has a **pot-bellied-pig** face because he gorges himself on cupcakes and blue raspberry popsicles.
- After working a **ten-hour** shift at Uncle Louie's Cafe, I craved a warm bath and a blue raspberry popsicle.

B. Numbers and fractions

- **Two-thirds** of the students had major errors in the class schedules. The counselor claimed in her **forty-one** years as a scheduler she'd never made a mistake. Oh, please.
- **One-fifth** of the junior class is going to the prom.

C. Some prefixes and some suffixes

- My **ex-boyfriend** is dating my **ex-best** friend.
- Who is **president-elect** of the chess club?

"These are sinful: acne, broken fingernails, chocolate, drugs, groupies, piracy, and sweat."

The Seven Deadly Sins

The Seven Deadly Sins of Writing

First Sin (Laziness): *Writing hideous sentences*

1. Sentence design: Remember from 'the Big 8' where we said that a sentence had to have a noun/pronoun plus a verb? We didn't mean you should stop there. Most of us don't talk in baby-talk sentences: *I have a dog. He is cute. My parents bought him for me. They think he's dumb. He pees on the floor. He chews up everything. Whatever.* So don't write that way. Write like you talk; use a mixture of complex and/or compound sentences. Check these out, the noun/pronoun and verb are in bold.

- When Angelica was fourteen, her **mother** and **father bought** her a French poodle.
- **Angelica named** her new puppy, Gaston, and **she spent** countless hours house training him.
- What **am I** to do with you, Gaston? **You must learn** to use the doggy door.
- **Angelica had** an idea. **She went** to the $1.99 Store and **bought** a plastic fire hydrant.
- **She placed** it in the middle of the backyard. **Gaston was thrilled,** and **Angelica was delighted** that Gaston learned to relieve himself outside.
- **Stop, Gaston! Those are** Grandma's dentures!

 *You Suck Uh-Oh!*

2. Sentence Fragments: (or sentences that are missing a noun/pronoun and/or a verb and don't express a complete thought.) To mend a fragment usually a word(s) must be added, appropriate punctuation, or a dependent word deleted.
- You can't buy fireworks in this state. Regardless of your age. *Regardless of your age* is a fragment.
- **CORRECT SENTENCE:** You can't buy fireworks in this state, regardless of your age.
- If dentists did not use drills. *The entire group of words is a fragment.*
- **CORRECT SENTENCE:** If dentists didn't use drills, people would not dread their check-ups.
- Austin likes sports cars. Particularly Ferraris and Corvettes. *Particularly Ferraris and Corvettes* is a fragment.
- **CORRECT SENTENCE:** Austin likes sports cars, particularly Ferraris and Corvettes. (Too bad Austin is only thirteen and can't drive.)

3. Diarrhea Sentences: Your sentence has the runs; it just runs on and on and on. Most English texts call these comma splices. It's just the runs and easy to fix. Usually, it simply needs the right punctuation.
- Dave broke his finger when the tennis racket slipped out of his hand the coach had warned him to tighten his grip he just didn't take her seriously. **(Really messy! Don't be lazy, clean it up!)**

- **CORRECT SENTENCES:** Dave broke his finger when the tennis racket slipped out of his hand. The coach had warned him to tighten his grip, and he just didn't take her seriously.

- Colter is eighteen-months-old and throws temper tantrums when he doesn't get his way his mother caters to his fits by picking him up kissing him and giving him cereal which stops his tantrum until he realizes that his mother is on the cell phone which gives him the opportunity to throw another fit stand in the corner take a poop in his diaper and toss yesterday's newspapers from the trash can. **(Can you smell the stink?)**
- **CORRECT SENTENCES:** Colter is eighteen-months old and throws temper tantrums when he doesn't get his way. His mother caters to his fits by picking him up, kissing him, and giving him cereal. This stops his tantrum until he realizes that his mother is on the phone. Then he throws another fit, stands in the corner, takes a poop in his diaper, and tosses yesterday's newspaper from the trash can.

Second Sin (Anger): *Composing disagreeable sentences*

It can be really ugly when there's no agreement. When sentences don't have agreement, they are grotesque! Agreement issues to consider:

1. Subject-verb Agreement:

singular subject + **singular verb** = agreement

plural subject + **plural verbal** = agreement

- *Gaston* **romps** across the yard in search of a fire hydrant.
- The *juniors* **have returned** from their class trip to Why, Arizona. (Why? Arizona?)
- Many *folks* at the baseball game **were booing** at the umpire.
- The *music* blasting from his stereo **annoys** the neighborhood.
- What **was** the *cause* of your bad-hair day?
- There **is** a *number* of reasons why Johnny is suspended from school. (No, *we* **are** not **sharing** the details about Johnny's love of spray paint.)

- **Tricky singular pronouns take singular verbs!**

anyone   anything   somebody   everything
no one   one   nothing   something
everyone nobody   neither   everybody
someone each   either   anybody

- **Does** *anyone* **want** to eat in the cafeteria? *Everyone* **complains** that *everything* **is** bad and **tastes** like cardboard.
- *Each* of tomatoes **was inspected** by the vegan patrol.
- *Neither* Austin nor Paul **is renting** a tux for the prom.
- *Nobody* **confronts** the bookstore lady; *everybody* **knows** she must have starred in a horror movie in her previous life.

Two or more subjects joined with *and* require a plural verb.

- *Tom, Anne,* ***and*** *Nancy* **are going** to Saturday detention.
- *Mindless homework **and** stupid word-search puzzles* **suck.**

2. Pronouns and Antecedent Agreement: Pronouns must agree in number and sex with the noun they replace—otherwise known as the antecedent.

- When the *cross country runners* returned from the regional meet, **they** were jazzed that the booster club had prepared a Chinese dinner for them.
- The *orange-chicken, chow mien* was cold, and **it** needed to be reheated. (Hey, I was too hungry to wait. I ate **it** anyway.)

> **WATCH OUT! TRICKY PRONOUNS BELOW!**

- *Neither* of the *boys* confessed **his** guilt in stealing catsup from the cafeteria.
- If *everything* has **its** place, why can't I remember **its** place?
- *Everyone* dreads **his** or **her** chemistry exam. (If one chooses not to use *his* or *her*, the sentence could be written: Most *students* dread **their** chemistry exams.)

3. Time Zone Agreement: Many writers intermix verb tenses. They begin writing an email, essay, or letter using present-tense verbs and shift--sometimes mid-sentence to past or future-tense verbs. Not only does this confuse the reader, but it screams, **"My writing sucks!"**

Imagine reading this paragraph:

> Yesterday I was babysitting a four-year-old, spoiled diva. After her nap, she will play dress-up in her mom's closet, so I called my boyfriend. We talked for about a half hour, and I never hear the child make a sound. Then I go check on her

and she's not in bed. She will be in the closet. She wasn't there! Now, I was worried, and I call her name. She comes out of her parents' bathroom with her hair covered in red nail polish! I think tomorrow I was fired.

Although the writer used the past tense *was babysitting, called, talked, wasn't, was fired,* the writer then changed to present tense *hear, go, call, comes, think,* and future tense *will play* and *will be.* As the reader, you've no idea whether this babysitter should ever be permitted to write again or be entrusted to a child's care.

When the **time** of the action actually changes from past, present, or future, shift the tense. Otherwise, keep it in the same time zone.

Third Sin (Greed): *Splitting hairs, not infinitives*

An infinitive is a verb form used after the word **to.** For example, **to read, to drink, to dance, to finish**

Some writers "split" the infinitive by adding another word between **to** and the verb **read, drink, dance, or finish.** The following are examples of split infinitives:

- Megan wanted to quickly read her book report.
- Juan tried to immediately eat his spaghetti and to simultaneously finish his math homework.

This split causes English teachers, editors, and grammarians **to seize** the red pen and **to scribble** scathing comments about how much the writer sucks!

The correct forms of these examples are:

- Megan wanted to read her book report quickly.

- Juan tried to eat spaghetti and to finish his math homework simultaneously. (Oops, the red spots!)

Fourth Sin (Lust): *Dangling your participles or misplacing your modifiers*

1. Dangling Participles: A participle is a verb, but in this case it acts like an adjective by describing a noun.

The girl **standing** there is my brother's significant other.

Standing is used to describe my brother's significant other.

Dangling a participle is similar to bungee jumping with a broken harness. Look these over and you will understand.

- Quietly munching hay, I watched the stallion in the pasture. *(Was I munching hay? I don't think so. The stallion was.)*
- **CORRECT SENTENCE:** I watched the stallion in the pasture quietly munching hay.
- While fiddling on the fiddle, Rome burned. *(Oh, really? Rome is a violinist?)*
- **CORRECT SENTENCE:** While Nero fiddled the fiddle, Rome burned.

2. Misplaced Modifiers: Simply put, a misplaced modifier is placing a word(s) in the wrong place at the wrong time. This is similar to buying a nonrefundable airline ticket that sells for 50% less the next day.

- I bought a car from a used car dealer with a leaky radiator. *(Excuse me. Does the dealer have a leaky radiator? If so, he needs **Depends**®.)*
- **CORRECT SENTENCE:** The car I bought from the used car dealer had a leaky radiator.

- She put the sandwiches back in the bag she had not eaten. *(Wow! She must have been really full not to have eaten the bag.)*
- **CORRECT SENTENCE:** She put the sandwiches she had not eaten in the bag.

- At the age of six, my family moved to Ohio. *(That's a feat for the record books.)*
- **CORRECT SENTENCE:** When I was six-years-old, my family moved to Ohio.

Fifth Sin (Envy): *Coveting unbalanced sentences*

Circus tightrope walkers like balance; they need balance, obviously. English teachers, and readers of English, like balanced writing. When sentences are awkward and unbalanced, they contain faulty parallelism. Equal ideas must be expressed in equal form.

- Kayla likes pretty dresses, expensive cosmetics, and shoes made in Italy.
- **Correct Sentence:** Kayla likes pretty dressy, expensive cosmetics, and Italian shoes.

- During our family vacation in Vietnam, we drank duck blood, ate something that resembled dog, and had diarrhea.
- **Correct Sentence:** During our vacation in Vietnam, we drank duck blood, ate dog meat, and had diarrhea. (What a nightmare!)

- You can get to Mexico by car, bus, or fly.
- **Correct Sentence:** You can get to Mexico by car, by bus, or by plane.

- My brother's fraternity house was filthy, disgusting, and reeked of vomit.

- **Correct Sentence:** My brother's fraternity house was filthy, disgusting and smelly.

Sixth Sin (Gluttony): *Eliminating obesity in writing and refraining from eating all of the Trick or Treat candy at one sitting*

Many writers think that the use of copious amounts of words (aka **deadwood**) make them sound smarter. It doesn't. KISS someone instead. (**K**eep **I**t **S**imple **S**tupid!)

AVOID	USE
at all times	always
at the present time	now
due to the fact that	as, since, because
in view of the fact that	as, since, because
in as much as	since
in the amount of	for
in the mean time	meanwhile
in the near future	soon
in the neighborhood of	nearly, about, around
in this place	here
previous to	before
there can be no doubt	doubtless
in reference to/or with regard to	about
rarely ever	rarely

Seventh Sin (Pride): *Being a doofus*

These are the most common errors that make you look like a doofus and will prevent you from advancing into the world of respected communication.

1. Using contractions in formal writing

In research papers, essays, and other formal documents, use cannot, it is, are not, they are, etc.

2. Using the word "you" in formal writing

As much as nursing is about administering medications and thorough patient assessments, it is also about the caring of the holistic patient; through meeting his/her physical, psychological, and spiritual needs. Most patients never remember the medications **you** gave them to save their lives, or **you** catching the early signs of a potentially-life threatening disease. They remember that **you** took the time to explain what was going on, made them feel safe, gave them a warm blanket, and held their hands when things got scary. *(Note the use of you in this college essay. The reader is saying, not me. I did not do those things. "You" antagonizes the reader.)*

3. There = not here (The parking lot is over *there*.) In formal writing it is best to avoid sentences that begin with there.

- **There** are many people that believe English is a difficult language to master.
- **Simplify it:** Many people believe that English is a difficult language to master.

4. Using multiple punctuation marks (???) or (!!!)
The multiple use of punctuation marks is for tweens and drama queens. One per customer, please.

5. **Misusing *bring* and *take***
Use bring when something is moved from far to near. Use take when something is moved from near to far.

Daddy **brings** home the bacon; Mommy **takes** his dirty laundry to the cleaners.

6. **Using *then* for *than* or vice versa**
   - Then refers to a sequence of events: I went to the gym, and **then** I went to get an ice cream cone.

   - Than is used in comparisons: Seniors are better **than** sophomores. (Well, not really. Seniors are just older **than** sophomores.)

7. **Misusing *lay* and *lie***
   - Use lay if someone is placing something somewhere: Momma **lays** her flyswatter on the counter. Momma **laid** her flyswatter on the counter. Momma **had laid** her flyswatter on the counter.

   - Use lie if someone or something is reclining: Momma **lies** in her bed until noon. Yesterday, Momma **lay** in her bed until noon. Momma **has lain** in her bed all week.

8. **Misusing *loose* (rhymes with goose) and *lose* (rhymes with shoes)**
   - Use loose if something is free or not tight: Anyone who has ever been around a goose knows the goose has **loose** bowels.

   - Use lose as a verb that means not win or misplace: My mother **loses** her car keys every morning.

9. Misusing *good* and *well* (Confusion arises because well can serve as an adjective meaning "good physical health" and as an adverb.)
- Now that the fever has broken, I feel **well** again.
- He plays the guitar **well**.
- I look **good** in blue.
- I'm feeling **good** about the math test. (Good refers to an emotional state, not physical state of health)

10. Misusing *bad* and *badly*
- I feel **bad** for the Arizona State Sun Devils. (The adjective bad describes the speaker's emotional health.)
- Their team played **badly**. (The adverb badly describes how the team played.)

But wait... there's more!

Unfortunately, English is filled with words that easily confuse all of us. These words are pronounced the same or nearly the same, but are **spelled** differently and have different **meanings**. Many word processing programs do not identify these errors in meaning when the word is spelled correctly. Imagine receiving the following emails:

- *Are school would like you to speak at career night and offer any advise you might have about prepositions concerning youth summer employment.*
- *Far two many trucks have break problems.*
- *Since I past the college entrance exam, I'd like to apply to you're university rather then the local community college.*

As a special bonus, we have included an extended list of words that confuse, bewilder or otherwise befuddle writers and the readers.

- **accept** *to admit or receive*
  except *exclude, excuse, or leave out*
  Kate wanted to **accept** the part-time job at *Popcorn Is Proper,* **except** she hated the smell of popcorn.

- **adapt** *to change or alter*
  adopt *to take or bring in*

  Ashley has **adapted** to Ms. Porker's teaching style, but she has yet to **adopt** Ms. Porker's snorts. (Thank-you, Ashley. Please, no snorting.)

- **advice** *something your Momma gives you*
  advise *to give guidance*

  Momma **advised** me to change my socks daily, but I never listened to her **advice**.

- **affect** *to cause something to change*
  effect *the result of the change*

  The **effects** of not changing his socks daily greatly **affected** Dave's relationship with his Momma.

- **are** *a verb form of to be*
  our *belonging to us*

  Our Momma swats mosquitoes on our patio, and we **are** going to get her a new swatter for Christmas.

- **beggar** *a person who asks for money, not to be confused with a dirt-bag friend*
  booger *a nasal substance that can be used as a snack or tossed at unsuspecting victims*
  bugger *a bad person*
  burger *a shortened form of hamburger until the inventions of veggie, tofu, gelatin, and chicken burgers*

As I waited outside the **burger** joint, a **beggar** approached me and asked for money. Since I'm not a **bugger**, I gave him a dollar and some change. After he shuffled away, my friends had yet to appear. I returned to my car, pulled down the visor mirror, checked my mascara, and surreptitiously searched my nasal cavities for **boogers**.

- **brake** *to slow down or stop or the mechanism that makes something slow down or stop*
  break *to destroy something or to rest*

  Meredith hit the **brakes** on her bicycle. She knew she'd **break** her ankle if she fell. With luck, she **braked** in time. After such an experience, she decided to take a **break**. She got off the wicked bike, grabbed her water bottle, and drank the limeade.

- **but** *except or to the contrary.* **NOTE: But always follows the positive comments about your performance on a test, on an essay, or on the athletic field.** **(AT)*
  butt *the end or one's posterior*

  I had been on the plane for three hours, and my **butt** was aching. I needed to stretch, **but** the captain had not turned off the "Fasten Seat Belt sign."

- **canvas** *weird material that is used in tents and such*
  canvass *acts of soliciting, collecting and surveying the opinions of the public*

  The artist's **canvas** depicted several young men **canvassing** their neighborhood for signatures to build a skate park.

- **capital** *the city that is home to state or federal government, first, or chief*
  capitol *the building housing state or federal government*

The **capitol** dome at Boise, Idaho's state **capital**, has the state motto engraved in **capital** letters. (And this is important?)

- **counsel** *to give advice or the person giving advice, e.g. your parent*
  council *a group of folk that guide a club or commission*

  The Student **Council counseled** the principal that the proposed cafeteria menu was awful. (Not all of the students wanted nuts and berries for lunch! Where is the grease?)

- **elicit** *to bring out*
  illicit *improper or yucky*

  Student Council **elicited** the opinions of all the students concerning the **illicit** behavior on the playground. (Hawker-spitting contests are yucky!)

- **hear** *to audibly be informed*
  here *in this place, not there*

  We're **here** at the box office waiting to **hear** if we still have reservations for the noon showing of *Revenge of the Booger Wars II*.

- **hole** *a cavity*
  whole *entire*

  She stuffed the **whole** package of dynamite down the gopher **hole**. Calmly, she lit the fuse and waited for those dastards to be blown to bits.

- **meet** *to encounter*
  meat *edible animal carcass*

When cannibals **meet** new explorers, they are overwhelmed with the prospect of fresh **meat**. (Yummy!)

- **passed** *completed, handed off, went by*
  past *not now*
  In **past** history, students did not have to **pass** tests to graduate from high school. They simply **passed** the requirements of their teachers and earned a diploma. (You should have graduated before the law **passed**.)

- **pedal** *a mechanism that uses a foot*
  peddle *to sell*

  Seth stepped on the gas **pedal** and sped to the swap meet. He couldn't wait to **peddle** his cure for athlete's foot. (Try washing your feet and wearing clean socks, and you won't need Seth!)

- **pore** *to study closely or the holes in one's skin*
  poor *substandard*
  pour *to flow freely*

  The sweat **poured** from the **pores** in his forehead. Brett had spent the night **poring** over his essay and knew he was going to get a **poor** grade. (Brett deserves a **poor** grade because he didn't read *English Doesn't SUCK: IT ROCKS!)*

- **principal** *balance on a debt, head poobah of a school, or chief*
  principle *a rule, law, or truth*

  Our high school **principal**, Mr. Arnholt, announced that all students would follow the **principles** of courtesy at football games.

- **road** *a dirt, gravel, or paved path used by pedestrians or vehicles*
  rode *yesterday's ride in or on a vehicle*
  rowed *yesterday's movement in an oar boat*

  Bruce **rode** his motorcycle down the country **road**. When he reached Campbell Lake, he parked the cycle, got in a dinghy, and **rowed** to the opposite shore. (Bruce must have had a girlfriend on the opposite shore, or why would he expend all the effort?)

- **role** *an actor or player's part*
  roll *a fancy piece of dough, to toss and turn, to beat a drum, to maneuver a plane in such a despicable fashion that one dirties his or her laundry*

  Each of the students was awarded a certificate for his or her **role** in winning the chess tournament. After a drum **roll**, each of the student's names was announced and applauded.

- **than** *a comparison word*
  then *relating to that time*

  When Paco discovered he was dumber **than** Isabella, he decided to copy her math homework. She discovered what he was doing. **Then** she schemed, plotted, and gave him all the wrong answers. (Isabella ROCKS!)

- **to** *toward or before a verb as to testify*
  too *also or excess amount*
  two *the number 2*

  For **two** years, he spent far **too** many hours playing video games, and he had **to** wear glasses. (Your Momma told you that would happen!)

- **trader** *a person who exchanges one thing for another*
  traitor *a bad person who betrays his wife, girlfriend, or country*
  Clark was a well-known fur **trader** among many Native American tribes. His buddy, Lewis, was tried as a **traitor** and hanged in the public square.

- **wear** *to be clothed, to erode, or clothing*
  where *in what place*

  "**Where** is the sock department," inquired Jack. "My socks are showing signs of **wear**, and I need a new pair to **wear** to the prom."

- **weather** *climate conditions*
  whether *if*

  Whether we go to the *Icky Doo* concert will depend on the **weather** advisory issued for thunderstorms and high winds.

"Something my garage band sorely lacked."

PWR

PWR

Before you paid good money to Vanna for a vowel, you'd have guessed this word. Yep, **power.** To become a better writer, you need to use **PWR (Prewriting, Writing, and Revising.)**

Prewriting

Prewriting includes finding a topic, drafting a topic sentence or thesis statement, and organizing ideas. Simply put: **Never write before you think.**

1. The topic
   - Sometimes you are assigned a topic about which to write.
   - However, if you have to come up with your own idea, write about what you know. If you've never swam naked in the ocean, don't write about it. If you and your thirteen-year-old friends stole the family car and went for a ride, that's a worthy story.
   - The best ideas come from brainstorming, doodling, making a list, or free-writing.

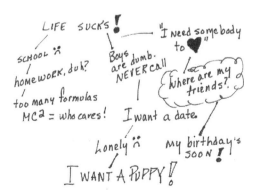

Doodling an Idea

If you're writing a paper comparing and contrasting two restaurants, a list may be helpful.

Making a list

McDoody's

McDoody's Phoenix   McDoody's Tokyo

Advertising focus: American cartoon characters	Advertising focus: Japanese anime
Architecture resembles 1950's diner	Architecture resembles tea house
Menu features: burgers, fries, shakes	Menu features: fish, noodles, rice, soups
Prices: Low to moderate	Prices: EXPENSIVE

2. After doodling or making a list, draft one sentence that contains your idea or **precise opinion** about the topic. This sentence is called a **topic sentence** for a paragraph or a **thesis statement** for an essay or research paper. Though the doodler had lots of thoughts, she wrote: *Dogs are great companions for single girls.* The lister wrote: *Though owned by the same conglomerate, McDoody's of Tokyo is vastly different from McDoody's of Phoenix.*

Writing

Past sections of this book have dealt with very basic writing. You've conquered the second level of *English Doesn't Suck: IT ROCKS* and still have lifelines. We know you're afraid you'll fall off the cliff, crash, and burn. Hold our hands as we lead you through the strategies and breeds of writing.

It is easier to outline your thoughts before writing using a simple format like the one below:

Topic Sentence/Thesis Statement: Dogs are great companions for single girls.

Supporting Evidence 1: Companionship

Details: Love me when no one else does

Supporting Evidence 2: Improve my social life

Details: Won't have to go out with stupid friends

       No more dumb boys

Supporting Evidence 3: Little dogs bring happiness

Details: Make me forget about formulas and homework

Closing/conclusion: Dogs are single girls' best friends.

There are two common ways organize your evidence: chronologically or emphatically.

- Chronological order is organization based on time, e.g. what happened first, second? what to do first, next, last?
- Emphatic order is arranged least to most important/most convincing evidence, e.g. a certain habit should stop because it's socially unacceptable, it makes a mess, and it can cause blindness. NOTE: **Always save the best**

reason for last, for that's what the reader will remember.

After completing her outline and considering organization, Bitsy wrote:

Dogs and Me

by Bitsy Blondell

Dogs are great companions for single girls. How do I know that? My life sucks! If I had a dog, I'd have companionship. Dogs are friends. My dog would love me. Even though I forget my homework and hate chemistry formulas. My dog would replace my friends. My friends party too much and never text unless they need a ride. Not to mention all those dumb boys that ask me out once and never call again!! If I had a dog, I would be sooo happy. Just a little dog. I wouldn't even mind cleaning up pee on the carpet. Dogs are single girls' best friends. If I can't get a dog, I'll get a kitten.

> **Gag us with a spoon, Bitsy. This is an awful piece of writing. It sucks! If you think it is great, see the revising section immediately.**

Writing Breeds

There is a ton of writing types from emails to research papers. Just like dogs, there are similarities and differences in each breed. Now that you can have conquered prewriting, outlining, and organizing, suck it up. Fasten your seat belt. We're moving on to the top four popular breeds.

1. Paragraph

2. Business Communications: including emails and letters

3. Essay

4. Research Paper

Paragraph

A paragraph is related group of sentences that discuss *one* idea.

How to write a paragraph

1. Topic sentence. This is usually the first sentence of the paragraph.

2. Evidence. Use examples and details to explain and convince the reader that your opinion is valid.

3. Closing sentence. This sentence brings finality to the paragraph.

Using the same format found in the appendix:

Topic Sentence: <u>Working as a restaurant bus boy was my worst job.</u>

Supporting Evidence 1: lousy pay

Details: minimum wage, no tips, $25 for four hours

Supporting Evidence 2: the work

Details: heavy, 30 pounds, vomit

Supporting Evidence 3: manager, Miss Louisa

Details: sexual harassment, pinching, touching, inviting to house

Closing sentence: I am done with bussing tables and being her boy.

Paragraph Example

    Working as a restaurant bus boy was my worst job. When I turned fifteen, I got a job at Uncle Louie's Cafe because I knew would be responsible for car insurance in one short year. I thought anyone could be a bus boy; it was a no-brainer. I was wrong. The pay was lousy. I received minimum wage, plus tips. Tips? Who on earth tips the bus boy after they have left the restaurant? Patrons usually don't see my work. Even though, the waiters and waitresses are supposed to share with me, most of them just pocketed the tips. On a great four-hour shift, I was lucky if I made $25. Further, bussing tables was not easy. A table of six could produce over thirty pounds of plates, bowls, silverware, and glasses. Once a fat kid gorged himself on all-you-can-eat spaghetti. When his chocolate sundae arrived at the table, he promptly vomited his undigested spaghetti and meatballs everywhere. Of course, it was my responsibility to clean up his spew. I gagged, gagged, and dry heaved, but somehow I managed to complete my work shift. However, the worst part of my job was dealing with my manager, Miss Louisa, a forty-something divorcee. At school, the teachers constantly harp on guys about sexual harassment. Teachers forget guys can also suffer sexual harassment, particularly if they work for Miss Louisa. When I was hired, she said, "you'll be my boy." I had no idea that being "her boy" meant she could pinch me, ask to see my biceps, or invite me to her condo after work. Wow, she was as old as my mother! I stayed at Uncle Louie's long enough to earn a year's worth of car insurance. The day I met my five-hundred-dollar goal, I quit. Miss Louisa emailed me and offered me a job at her new restaurant, but I said no. I am done with bussing tables and being her boy.

Business Communications

Unless you have inherited Great Aunt Lucy's fortune, you **must master** this section. Without skills in business writing, you will spend your miserable life begging Mother Hubbard for a promotion.

Email

Mosquito bites kill; email kills. A poorly-written email can be fatal to a contract, a business transaction, or a career, as malaria is to a third world country.

How to write an email

1. Think. Email is deadly because it's **immediate, public, and permanent**. In an instant, you can reply to an inquiry, ask a question, or break off a relationship; within seconds, you can receive a response. Your message can be forwarded to thousands across the network world. Even the sheik of a remote kingdom will know you are stupid! Thus, it is **critical** that you think before you write.

2. Draft. Yes, your computer, cell phone, or other electronic device will allow you to write a draft of your response to an angry customer or your boss. The draft should contain brief, clear, logical sentences or bullet points that use professional business terms. A professional response *does not include*: BTW, OMG, WTF, :) or :(.

3. Wait. After at least 15 minutes have passed, open your draft and reread. Does your communication make sense? Have you used the right words, have you asked logical questions, have you proposed viable solutions? Are dates, times, monetary amounts correct? If you are satisfied, run spell check.

4. Send. Once you hit send; it's gone. If you made an error, it could be lethal. You may be shoveling dog doo for his Highness.

Email Example

Dr. Jensen:

On behalf of the freshmen class of Butte High School, I extend an invitation for you to participate in our October 12, 2011, career-day seminar.

We offer you:

- consultation fee of $2.99 per day
- lodging at the Sky Dive Inn
- meals in the school cafeteria
- transfers to and from the Sanford County Airport

Please let me know if you can join us for this very important event.

Thank-you,

Byrd Jae Onion, Class President

Butte High School

Letters

Even in this hi-tech world, business letters are used both professionally and personally. Your job may demand that you initiate communication or respond to clients. At home, you may need to confirm a telephone conversation or send a letter of complaint. Though this breed of writing requires less time-sensitive action, it still demands rational thinking.

How to write business letters

1. **Draft a single sentence that states the purpose of the letter.**
   - Please consider my enclosed application and essay for admittance into your university.
   - I have received and reviewed your request to raise the limit on your credit card from $125 to $2,500.

2. **Draft the supporting details.** Dates, facts, evidence, and/or examples

3. **Follow stodgy format rules.** (Grow up! Every once in a while it is necessary to play by the rules; you can't be a sixth grader forever.)
   - Heading includes your address and date. No, you don't rewrite the address if you're using the company letterhead.
   - Inside address, which is the name and address of the people you're writing.
   - Greeting, such as Dear Mrs. Higgenbottom, Dear Sir, To Whom It May Concern, followed by a colon (:)
   - Body of letter arranged in paragraph form
   - Closing, such as Sincerely, Respectfully yours, Yours truly.
   - Your signature, followed by your typewritten name below.

Business Letter Example

1004 North Crenshaw
Durham, Ohio
October 24, 2010

Mighty Mikes Inc.
1210 N. Madison
New York, New York 10230

Dear Sir or Madam:

I purchased your Mighty Mike, model 129-01, and it came with a full, money-back guarantee if not completely satisfied. I am returning because I am not satisfied. Your "revolutionary" microphone advertisement stated that "any voice could be changed to sound like a rock star's voice." However, when I plugged it into my amplifier and began to sing, I still sounded like Bambi Bernardo with a cold. All of my friends on the basketball team laughed when I tried to perform a patriotic melody at the pep assembly. They even took up a collection to get me voice lessons!

I have suffered embarrassment for my high, squeaky voice my entire life. I have tried elixirs, salves, and syrups, none of which have lowered my voice. Your company's promise just seemed to be the miracle for which I had been hoping. Your mike didn't deliver. Please return my money.

Thank you for your attention to this matter.
Sincerely,

Brutus Baxter

The Essay

Essay? Yes, essay. We know that word has caused you to dirty your boxers. Go change your undies, pour yourself a soda, and read on. Essays have less-threatening aliases. They are known as papers, reports, stories, and articles. An essay is nothing more than a bunch of paragraphs that relate to **one** topic.

Essays contain three parts:

- Introduction or the **first** paragraph to get the reader interested. It contains the thesis statement.
- Body or a minimum of **three** paragraphs that provide evidence and examples. Each of these paragraphs have one topic sentences that discusses only one topic. (The size of this section can vary.)
- Conclusion or **last** paragraph that summarizes and restates the thesis. This paragraph does **NOT** include any new information that was not previously discussed in the body.

Essay Outline

Introduction and Thesis Statement: Washington needs to be closed and demolished.

Body Paragraph 1

  Topic Sentence: The school is in need of expensive renovation that would far exceed the cost of building a new school.

Supporting Evidence:

Details: windows, lighting, furnace, gym

Body Paragraph 2

Topic Sentence: Secondly, the cafeteria and auditorium may have once been "technological wonders" ninety years ago,

Supporting Evidence:

Details: warming ovens, furniture, sound, lighting, storage

Body Paragraph 3

Topic Sentence: However, the worst thing about Washington is its continued use.

Supporting Evidence:

Details: Too many staff, students have to use dismal place

Conclusion and restatement of the thesis: Due to the high cost of renovation, the conditions of the cafeteria and auditorium, and the overall environment for students and staff, Washington should be torn down.

Essay Example

Washington School Sucks

by Taron Downs

Washington School was built in the early 1920's before the infamous Stock Market Crash. When it opened, the local newspaper proclaimed it "a modern, technological wonder." Unfortunately, ninety years have passed, and it remains in use. Washington needs to be closed and demolished.

The school is in need of expensive renovation that would far exceed the cost of building a new school. All of the windows and light fixtures need to be replaced. The oil heating system is so inefficient that students and teachers are forced to wear coats and gloves during the winter. Due to a series of leaky roofs, the gymnasium floor heaved and warped. The cost to replace the floor was astronomical, so school officials simply declared it unfit for use and locked the entrance doors. Thus, the students must hold practices at neighboring school gyms, and physical education classes are held outside when the weather permits.

Secondly, the cafeteria and auditorium may have once been "technological wonders" ninety years ago, but today the cafeteria is nothing more than a myriad of warming ovens for frozen pizza, tater bites, and chicken fingers. The wooden chairs and tables are etched with the names of couples that have been dead for years and with rude comments about long-gone principals. The auditorium's sound system is nonexistent. The lighting and curtain riggings were damaged by another leaky roof, and the dressing rooms have been turned into textbook storage areas.

However, the worst thing about Washington is its continued use. Every September, 600 students and 40 staff members walk the halls, sit in classrooms, and eat in the cafeteria. All of these people are subjected to dismal disrepair, inadequate heating and lighting, and musty odors. Simply stated: it is not an environment conducive to educating students for 21st Century skills.

Due to the high cost of renovation, the conditions of the cafeteria and auditorium, and the overall environment for students and staff, Washington should be torn down. Following its demolition, it can be replaced with a cherry orchard.

Essay Styles

Before writing an essay, the author must answer the question: What is its **purpose?** There are seven common methods or arrangements of essays.

1. **Narration**= tells a story
   - An example might be: The day I got my driver's license was the happiest day of my life.
   - Organized chronologically

2. **Argumentation/Persuasion**= to convince or persuade to a particular point of view or to strengthen or change the attitude of the reader. It is not a fanatical, unreasonable approach.
   - Topic must be controversial enough to have a difference of opinion.
   - Organized emphatically—Save the BEST argument for last

3. **Compare/Contrast**= an examination of two or more things in order to establish similarities or differences. An analogy is an extended comparison: My life is a roller coaster.

4. **Cause/Effect**= a cause is a force, action, or influence that produces an effect. It is the reason something happens. An effect is the result or product of a cause. It is whatever happens or what will happen if.
   - Organized emphatically
   - When writing about the cause and effect relationship, the writer can reason in several ways--causes and effects of WWII, or effect to cause (Why did it happen?), or cause to effect (What will happen if I don't pass the college entrance exam? What are the effects of dropping out of school.)

5. **Process**= a series of actions, changes, functions, steps, or operations that bring about a particular result.

- Informational (How does it happen? How does it work? An example might be: How a body is embalmed or an explanation of an Amish wedding ceremony.)
- Instructional (How do I do it? An example might be: How to make Grandma's stuffed cabbage rolls.)
- Organized chronologically (What happens first, second, third.)

6. Description=specific details to create a clear picture of something or someone
- Usually organized spatially—top to bottom, left to right, far to near

Detailed description of each of these modes follows on the next pages. Suck it up. Turn the page.

Narrative Paper

A narrative paper tells or recounts a story and is arranged chronologically. The paper answers the questions: who, what, when, where, why, and how.

How to write a Narrative

1. Think of an-**est** experience--something that stirred strong feelings and created a lasting meaning: scari**est**, happi**est**, sadd**est,** sick**est,** funni**est,** m**ost** embarrassing.

2. Now if your happi**est experience** was a two-week vacation in Hawaii, narrow your topic. No one wants to read a day-by-day account of your trip, just as no one wants to sit through a four-hour slide show of your pictures. **Draft** a topic sentence, such as: *To climb Diamondhead is an exhilarating experience.*

3. Determine point of view. Will the paper be written from the first person perspective or "I"? Or from the third person perspective, "he/she/they."
- "I" narratives are limited to the actions and events seen through the eyes of **one** person.
- "He/she/they" narratives are omniscient, like someone perched high above the action watching and recording. These narratives allow the writer to portray events from various angles and reveal the thoughts and actions of all.

4. Use vivid verbs and rich language to carry the story, such as wobble, stagger, smack, crash, loiter, grumbled, stammered

5. Use rich dialogue to reveal emotion and personality--not he said/she said, but words such as, yelled, screamed, growled, answered, whispered, stated, stammered, responded, cried.

Remember to start a new paragraph each time the speaker changes.

6. Write a conclusion that brings closure to the story. This is **NOT** a "to be continued" soap opera, and "the end" is not an appropriate conclusion.

Narrative

To Pepe, with Love

by Makenzie Mastiff

June 2, 2010, was the worst day of my life. School had been out for almost two weeks, and I was already bored. I missed my friends, I missed Mr. Arnholt's history class, and I even missed the greasy tater tots in the cafeteria. My parents had taken my brother, Bruce, and me to spend the weekend at my grandparents' cabin--far away from upscale malls, movie theaters, and internet access. Even my cell phone reception was compromised. I was suffering from city separation and too much family interaction, especially obnoxious, Bruce. Tomorrow we would return to suburbia; I could not wait!

"Makenzie, Makenzie? It is almost dinner time," called Grandma. "Come and help me set the table."

Reluctantly, I earmarked the page in a fashion magazine, lifted myself from the porch swing, and went off to assist my grandmother. The last supper was delicious. The fried chicken was crispy, the homemade rolls were fabulous, and the strawberry pie was delectable. As I put the remaining dirty silverware in the dishwasher, I looked at clock. In less than two hours, we would be headed back to the city!

"How can I kill some time?" I wondered. I was so stuffed and needed exercise. "Hey, Bruce, do you want to play ball?" Now, I already knew that the prince of gluttony would find my request absurd. He only exerted himself to cram gobs of candy, ice cream, and potato chips into his mouth. Someday, he would regret all of the pussy pimples that would erupt as a result of his eating habits.

"No way," responded the fatso, ten-year-old. "I want more pie."

"Ball? Did you say ball?" My grandmother's wire-haired fox terrier, Pepe, seemed to ask. "Of course, I wanna play ball. Look at me see me jump up and down and wag my tail. Let's go, Mack! Let's go play ball."

"Come on, Pepe. We'll play ball." The dog exuberantly followed me out to the shed where I found an old wooden bat and a decrepit softball. I tossed the ball in the air several times and attempted to hit it. Of course, I missed. Pepe was frustrated. She was not having fun. Then I threw the ball in the air. As it came down, it connected to my swung bat. Pepe was on the run. She turned to face the ball. I screamed!

The ball smacked Pepe directly between her eyes. She stumbled and fell to the ground. "Oh, no!" I cried. Tears were running down my face; had I killed beloved Pepe? I was dizzy; sweat poured from my face. I was shaking uncontrollably; I was about to vomit as the family came rushing from the house and the back porch. Was Pepe dead? Had I committed murder? Would I be sentenced to a humane society jail for the rest of my life?

Bruce was screeching, "Mack killed Pepe. Mack killed Pepe." That was just what I needed: taunts from the brat prince. If anybody deserved to die that evening, it was him. The betrayer of secrets, the king of calories, the toad who loved pie more than baseball!

Finally, Pepe stood. She was stunned. Her eyes were dazed. She wobbled toward me and began to lick my sweaty toe. I plopped down on the ground, petted her wildly, and gave thanks for her resurrection. "I'm so sorry. I love you, Pep. I will always love you. You're my best puppy."

Now, four years later, Pepe and I play baseball with tennis balls. Bruce has a raging case of acne. Life is good.

Argumentation or Persuasion Paper

We won't lie. This is a **very** difficult paper to write, for its purpose is to convince or change the reader's attitude about a controversial issue. The writer must be definitive and passionate, without being disrespectful, and the writer cannot be fanatical nor unreasonable. Unlike much of life, this paper calls for sanity, facts, and logical thinking.

How to write Argumentation

1. Determine a debatable point, which is a point that can't be proved or disproved by fact.

- Debatable points must be clear, not vague nor wishy-washy, such as *Sometimes marijuana should be legalized, and sometimes it shouldn't.* (The reader has no idea which side you support.)
- Bad debatable points: *Skiing is fun. I love oatmeal. Women live longer than men (statement of fact that is not debatable.)*
- Good debatable points: *Illegal immigration should be enforced. High schools place too much emphasis on competition.*

2. Determine the opposing arguments, for the proverb is correct: *There are two sides to every story.* The opposition should be acknowledged.

3. Gather convincing evidence, such as facts, statistics, verifiable evidence, and examples.

4. Organize evidence from least to most important evidence. Save the most compelling argument for last, for that's the one the reader will remember.

5. **Draft paper using the third person** (he/she/one/they.)

You Suck Uh-Oh!

Never use " you" for in formal writing. Avoid using "I" because the focus should be on the topic, not the writer.

6. **Draft a conclusion.**

Persuasion Paper

Lend Me Your Ear

by Will E. Tell

"One for all and all for one," proclaimed the Three Musketeers. Famous quotations about the value of sharing abound. Parents continually urge us to share with our brothers and sisters. Teachers encourage us to share our work with peer evaluators. Even the guidance counselor asks us to share our opinions about block schedule, the cafeteria food, and the new dress code. Selfish as it may sound, sharing is not a good thing.

Sharing causes illness. Far too many people share personal, hygiene products with others. In this world of bird flu, swine flu, cat flu, and worm flu, disease is easily transmitted. As reported in a national television expose, Chantilly shared her high-volume mascara with her friend. Within two days, Chantilly's voluminous eyelashes were reduced to stubs. Jordan shared her high-gloss, lip liner and then applied it to her own lips. Immediately, a large, greenish-yellow, oozing boil appeared. Bob shared his comb with a random student. When Bob combed his sideburns at lunchtime, he fell to the ground! He wriggled around and screamed "meow, oink, and tweet," until the ambulance arrived.

Secondly, one should never share favorite possessions. Harold had saved his allowance to buy an original copy of *Meteor Man Meets the Giant Ferret* comic book; it was the prize of his collection. His little sister begged to take it to school for show-and-tell. Harold relented and reluctantly gave it to his sister. When she returned the comic, two pages were missing! She and her friends had used the pages to make a poster for an art project. Butch Malone lent his letter jacket to Austin. Austin left it in the back seat of his unlocked, car. Austin's car was stolen, and while the car was found, the jacket was not. Annie and her family went to San

Diego for the weekend. Annie's boyfriend, Andrew, had tickets to the Scorpions concert the same weekend. Unfortunately, Annie suggested Andrew take her best friend, Jaimie, to the concert. Andrew and Jaimie are now going steady, and Annie's back is still peeling from sunburn.

While one should refrain from sharing hygiene products and possessions, the worst sin one can commit is the sharing of secrets. Regardless, if it is prefaced with, "If you repeat this, I'll have to kill you," once the secret is shared; it is no longer a secret. DUH! Maria is a reformed, secret sharer. Six weeks ago, Jack texted her, "goin to ask Meg to prom! shes hotttttt! dont tell." Maria was beside herself. Should she tell Meg? Should she just wait till Jack popped the question? Maria decided to share, and Meg was ecstatic! Meg spent the next few days dreaming about Jack, the prom, the dress, the flowers, the limo ride, and the romance. In the meantime, two other guys asked her to the prom, which she promptly refused; she waiting for Jack. Jack asked his lab partner, Christie, to the prom; Meg sat home alone. Maria, Jack, and Meg no longer speak to each other. Maria went to secret-sharing rehab and learned techniques to control her inner urge to tell secrets.

Contrary to mainstream opinion and advice, sharing is unhealthy, leads to heartache, and destroys friendships. Of course, it is okay to share knowledge and experience. It is not okay to share toothbrushes, straws, nor underwear. It is not okay to share a designer shirt with someone whom is three sizes larger. It is really, really, really not okay to share something that someone told in confidence, complete with a "cross your heart" promise. When Jessica finds out that her best friend told another girl that Jessica said that the other girl was...Uh OH. A thunderstorm is about to happen. Run for cover!

Compare and Contrast Paper

The compare and contrast paper is the examination of two or more things in order to establish their similarities and/or differences. This examination is used in daily lives to make choices between alternatives, such as which bottle of cologne to purchase or which person to date. This is the **most** common type of essay assignment.

How to write Compare and Contrast

1. First decide on two or more things to be examined: *playing versus studying, candidate platforms, before my parents' divorce/after their divorce.*

2. Draft a topic sentence: *The platforms of student council candidates, Bob Doowah and Sandra Smuck are similar and different.*

3. Discuss the similarities: *Opinions on the homecoming parade and tailgate party, lunch-hour intramural sports, and cafeteria services*

4. Discuss the differences: *Opinions on community service, use of cell phones, and increased ticket prices for events*

5. Write a conclusion.

How to write Compare OR Contrast

Often, things are only evaluated based on similarities **or** differences. For example, *There are several similarities between McDoody's menu and Bigger Burger's menu.* In other evaluations, differences are the focal point, such as *My life drastically changed when my parents went bankrupt, or boys'* *sports are better than girls' sports.* There are two ways to arrange compare or contrast papers.

1. One side at a time (This format is frequently used in before and after scenarios.)

- Introduction with a topic sentence
- Before my parents went bankrupt or boys' sports
- After my parents went bankrupt or girls' sports
- Conclusion

2. Point-by-point (This format is frequently used in making decisions.)

- Introduction with a topic sentence: *When I moved from Youngstown, Ohio, to Phoenix, Arizona, I discovered many differences in the two cities. The weather, the educational opportunities, and the people were strikingly different.*
- Discuss weather in Ohio vs. Arizona
- Discuss educational opportunities in Ohio vs. Arizona
- Discuss people in Ohio vs. Arizona *(Yes, there is a difference.* **Phoenix young men are adorable.)** *(AT)
- Conclusion

Contrast Paper

The Interesting Lives of Mosquitoes

by Bugs R. Kuhl, PhD

OMG, it's summer time! For many parts of America, summer time is synonymous with mosquito time. According to entomological research, the critter responsible for the most human deaths worldwide is the pesky mosquito. Unlike humans, it is difficult to simply pull down the genes and see the differences between boy and girl mosquitoes. However, there are significant differences between the mosquito sexes.

Though all mosquitoes have one pair of wings, six legs, and two eyes that allow them to see in multiple directions at once, boy mosquitoes are smaller than girl mosquitoes. Boy mosquitoes do not make the dreaded buzzing sound, and boy mosquitoes do not bite humans. Their proboscis is not ragged; thus instead of chomping a blond woman, wearing a black shirt, whom has recently eaten a banana, boys prefer to spend their ten to twenty days on earth drinking nectar from flowers and courting girl mosquitoes.

In direct contrast, girl mosquitoes are femme fatales. These deadly ladies buzz in one's ear, delight in attacking children during a full moon, and thrive on sucking blood. Their serrated proboscis allows them the pleasure of siphoning blood from victims. Since a girl mosquitoes' life span can reach 100 days, their threat can last an entire summer. Further, the saliva of mosquitoes is said to contain some of the same ingredients found in rat poison.

Mosquitoes are the most dangerous critters on earth. Folks must beware of them--particularly the female ones. Like most female species on earth, girl mosquitoes live longer, talk a lot, and can suck anyone dry.

Cause and Effect Paper

A cause is an action, force, or influence that produces an effect. An effect is the result or product of a cause. *I overslept **(cause)** and missed the final exam **(effect)**.* When writing about the cause and effect relationship, the writer can reason in two ways: Effect-to-cause(s) or cause-to-effect(s).

Effect to Cause(s) Reasoning

This reasoning is better known as **Momma's reasoning**, for it answers the question why? Why'd you do dat? Why'd dat happen?

Effect = dropping out of high school

- Why did he or she drop out of high school? What caused him or her to drop out?
- List and explain the causes: got bored, found a decent job (doubtful), went to work, hung out with friends, etc. **(If you are contemplating dropping out of high school, you are stupid.)** *(AT)

Cause to Effect(s) Reasoning

This reasoning answers the questions : What are the results? What will happen if?

Cause = dropping out of high school

- What are the results of dropping out? What will happen if one drops out of high school?
- List and explain the effects: Did or will disappoint family and self, Did not or will not earn a diploma, Did or will earn less money than those with diplomas in

particular work field, Did or will be a **doofus forever,** etc.

NOTE: Take any event, situation, or incident and reason either effect to causes or cause to effects, for example, a car accident. Why did the accident happen? (Effect to causes) **Or** What were the effects/results of the accident? (Cause to effects) Further, some essay questions ask for both causes and effects, e.g. What were the three major causes and three major effects of the American Civil War?

> ***BEWARE: Faulty Reasoning Ahead***

Sometimes an examination of the cause/effect relationship is flawed, and these flaws have fancy Latin names. Behold these flaws:

- My boy friend and I had a fight, and the earthquake hit. Our spat must have caused the earth to move.
- A black cat crossed in front of the oncoming car, and moments later the right tire blew. Drat, those black cats.
- Because Julie had a goodnight's sleep, she aced her eye exam.
- James is a fabulous football player; he'll make a great college student.
- If we can build cars, we can stop terrorism.
- **Politicians/ dropouts engage in faulty reasoning on a routine basis. *(AT)**

Effect to Causes

Life Sucks

by Moe Skeeter

"Hello, America! I'm Sara Swartz on assignment in Latimer, Iowa. Tonight, I am interviewing three teens whom believe their life sucks because they are teenagers. Stay tuned for my full report."

Anyone between the ages of 13 through 19 knows that being a teenager sucks! It sucks in varying degrees from suck to suckiest. Eighteen and 19-year-olds are out of school and in college, in the military, or in the workforce and can vote. Since they soon will pass over to the other side, some aspects of their lives simply suck. Sixteen and 17-year-olds can drive, go on dates, and attend the prom. However, they are still in school and have curfews; their lives are suckier. Thirteen to fifteen-year-olds have the suckiest lives because their only reward is being labeled a teenager. Matt, Lindsay, and Justin know their lives suck because they are teens.

Matt is 18 and works full-time at Bender Auto Shop as a mechanic's helper. "My job sucks," he states. "After I graduated from high school, my parents told me to go to college full-time or get a job. School was the last place I wanted to be, so I got a job to pay for car insurance, gas, and entertainment." According to Matt, he quickly discovered that working in a menial job at minimum wage was awful. His boss, Drew, is a sloth who orders him to do all of the grimy, greasy tasks, and Drew often shorts Matt's paycheck by $50 a week. Matt wants to rid himself of dirty fingernails and oily odor, but his car insurance rate increased again. He is stuck in a morass of debt and a slave job at 18. Matt laments, "Sara, make me famous. I know I'm young, but help me get my miserable life together."

Lindsay says she's 16 and a half, and she's a varsity cheerleader, vice president of the junior class, and a member of the drama club. Her life sucks because her boyfriend just broke up with her. "Brittany used to be my best friend. Then I caught her making out with my boyfriend under the bleachers. Bobby, my boyfriend, denied it. He said it wasn't anything; he said it meant nothing. Then, he sent a skanky text message to my cell phone about how he needs his freedom. He wants to be free to hang with the guys, and he's sick of the cheer bimbos. As if the cheerleaders are bimbos. Take a look in the mirror, Bobby!" Lindsay also thinks school sucks, particularly Mrs. Johnson's English class. "Old Lady Johnson is forever talking about dead white men, like Mark Twain, F. Scott whatever, and Carl Stupid Sandburg. I mean, who in his right mind would stop by a snowy, woods and miss their favorite TV show? Further, get a life. Horses are not queer. Would you not agree, Sara?" Indeed, Lindsay believes that being 16 and one-half sucks.

Justin is fourteen-years-old and readily admits that it sucks to be a teen. However, unlike the others, Justin arrives at the convenience store on his skateboard or bicycle; while Matt parks his vintage, muscle car, and Lindsay dodges her Mom's convertible around the gas pumps. Now Matt and Lindsay are not followed by the clerk around the store. Justin is. He was made to turn in his backpack upon entry. His companions were made to remain outside, for the store sign demands, " ONLY ONE STUDENT AT A TIME." Justin takes offense at the sign but knows if he objects, he will be banished from the Qwickie Pickie Mart forever. "Sara, I have money. I just want one of those high-energy drinks. You know, Blue Calf. I want one of those all-day-long-broiled, hot dogs. Yet, that clerk skulks around me like I'm going to steal a candy bar. Like, why would I do that? I hate chocolate. Why am I being treated like some potential shoplifter?"

The insights shared by these teens indicate there are degrees of suck. When Sara posed her final question to the interviewees:

What really, really, sucks about being a teenager? Their response was unanimous.   Acne.

"Sara Swartz reporting live. Details at 11."

Process

Sometimes this arrangement is referred to as a nightmare! Most kids have experienced the horror of buying an unassembled bookcase, bicycle, or new computer program,. As they begin to read the assembly pamphlet or download the instructions, they query, "And where are the missing screws that are needed to fit part A with part B?" A process paper may be:

- Instructional or informational
- If it is instructional, do **not** write about something that you have **never** executed yourself. If you've never cheated on a test nor stolen a candy bar from the convenience store, you'll have difficulty persuading the reader that you are an expert. Choose a topic that you know how to execute. Further, your "how-to" instructions must be clearly understood by the reader at his/her **first** reading.
- If it is informational, such as how to embalm a body, you'll probably need to research the steps in the process. (Unless of course, you are a vampire.)
- Usually organized chronologically--what happens first, second, etc.

How to write a process paper

1. Draft a topic sentence. For example, *Have you ever wanted to be a nerd but were afraid to try? You need only to have the right equipment and behave in the prescribed manner, and you, too, can be a nerd.*

2. Next, clearly delineate the materials needed. *To be a nerd, one would need: a pocket protector full of pens stuffed into a checkered shirt pocket, high-water black pants, black-rimmed glasses held together with white, adhesive tape.*

3. Enumerate steps. *Once you are dressed like a nerd, you are ready to act like a nerd in both the work place and social situations. At work you must....*
At a party you must....

4. Write a concluding statement. *After you have the necessary attire and mastered the appropriate behaviors in both the work place and social situations, anyone who meets you will know you are a nerd.*

Process

It Is Easy to be Weird

by I. B. Jamen

Have you ever wanted to be a nerd or a geek, but were afraid to try? By following very simple steps, you can achieve success. You need only to secure the proper clothing and the correct behaviors for school and for social situations. You, too, will be transformed as the epitome of doofism.

First, you must go to a thrift store to select the proper wardrobe. Young men should scour the clothing racks for polyester trousers that are at least one inch shorter than their ankles. Plaid shirts with one pocket are a must, for the pocket must be filled with mechanical pencils and pens. White or argyle socks, black-rimmed glasses held together with white, adhesive tape, and black sturdy shoes should be purchased to complete the outfit. Young women should choose polyester skirts and dresses, a variety of hair bows and barrettes, knee socks, and simple, white tennis shoes. Winged glasses and a drab, green backpack may also be used to accentuate any attire.

After donning your new clothes and accessories, you must adopt appropriate behaviors for educational settings. Always come to class with textbooks, notebook paper, plenty of writing implements, calculators, rulers, scissors, and glue. Fellow students will be amazed by your preparedness. When the teacher asks a question, raise your hand immediately. If you are not called on, wave your hand back and forth, and make "uh, uh" sounds. Never answer a question with a simple, yes or no. Expound on the underlying reasons for your choice. Again, your classmates will marvel at your intellect. Finally, stay after class and talk with the teacher. Offer to organize papers, to collect teaching materials, and to fix her computer or to build her a new one.

While the mastery of school behavior is necessary to your success in geekdom, it is most important in social settings, such as football games and parties. When attending an athletic event, wear team colors. While spectators are enthralled in the game, run up and down the bleachers with friends. Talk loudly about global warming, sustainability, and your physics project. Toss popcorn at cute girls or guys. At parties, do not hide in the corner. Join a group of the opposite sex and tell a joke, similar to: *Why was 6 afraid of 7? Because 7,8,9.* After delivering the punch line, snort in laughter. Practice snorting until you perfect it, or your jokes will not be well-received. When refreshments are served, recite authoritatively the bad ingredients and calorie count of potato chips, pizza, and cola products. Suggest the hosts serve green vegetables and skim milk. At the close of the party, invite the attendees to your house to see your Lego® collection of famous historical landmarks.

Being a nerd or a geek is easy. With the proper clothing and behaviors, you can establish your reputation as the kid most likely to succeed in science, technology, and mathematics. At your ten-year, high school reunion, everyone will remember your name: Will or Wilma Doors.

Informational Process Paper

(An informational process paper answers the question: How is it done? This type of process does not emphasize the reader's role in executing a task.)

The Amish Way

by Gladys Knotme

The wedding rite is based on religious and cultural tradition. A typical Protestant wedding ceremony may last fifteen minutes, while a Catholic ceremony might exceed an hour. In the Amish culture, weddings are a lengthy process.

Following a secret courtship, the deacon announces the impending marriage at a church service. After the announcement, the bridegroom-to-be must personally visit all wedding guests to invite them to the ceremony. Every morning he hitches up his horse and buggy and sets off. Since usually two hundred or so folk are invited, it may take the bridegroom several days to accomplish this task.

On the day before the wedding, as many as thirty men and women gather to prepare the wedding feast. It is considered an honor to be asked to assist in this endeavor. Breads and desserts are baked, potatoes are peeled, vegetables are cooked, and meats are roasted. Further, custom demands that the bridegroom cut the heads off all of the ducks, turkeys, and chickens to be served at the feast.

The couple and their invited guests arrive at the church before 9:00 a.m. on the wedding day. The four-hour ceremony includes preaching and questioning of the couple. At 12:30 PM, the bishop calls the couple forward, asks each of them several questions, and then blesses their union. Afterward, the couple and guests return to the family home, and the feast begins.

Amish weddings are laden with cultural nuances and religious beliefs. As in other religious faiths, the Amish wedding rite is a celebration with family and friends. However, issuing personal invitations, slaying of fowl, and attending a four-hour church service clearly delineate the "Amish way."

Description Paper

A descriptive paper creates and clarifies a vivid, sensual picture for the reader. Thus, it relies heavily on the five senses: taste, smell, touch, hearing and sight. It is filled with details and can be organized spatially--top to bottom, left to right, far to near.

Using your five senses, evaluate this ramshackle. Can you convince developers through an email that this house should not be demolished because it was a stop on the Underground Railroad? If you parents inherited this property, can you convince them that it is worth saving? If this is your grandparents' former home, can you describe your memories on the back porch, under the tree, or in the upstairs bedroom?

How to write Description

1. Determine the subject and write a topic sentence: *Our family homestead should be donated to the Vernon Volunteer Fire Department.*

2. Buy a thesaurus. It abounds with sensual words and won't bother your queasy stomach nor lack thereof.

3. Use vivid words and examples to justify your position: *The foul-smelling, bat droppings on the second floor would have gagged a maggot.*

4. Write a concluding statement.

Description

What Seems Often Does Not Equal What Is

by Lindsay Leader

"Jen. You'll never believe it. Guess who asked me out?" I texted.

"Who?" Jen texted.

"Steven Gorgeous Brown!"

"IURD." Translation: In Your Dreams, Jen wrote.

Yes, it is true. Steven Brown, captain of the football team, asked me to go to the movies with him on Saturday night. I had only two days to get ready. Where would I start? After school on Thursday, I went to the trendy mall in Cookstown. I went from upscale boutiques to national department stores searching for the perfect outfit. I tried on outrageous print sundresses; low-rider skirts; filmy, v-neck blouses; black, capri pants; and countless pairs of over-priced jeans. As I stood in the dressing rooms staring myself in the mirror, I decided I needed to lose weight, to get a haircut, and to have my make-up professionally done. After all, I had a date with S. Gorgeous Brown! Three hours had passed before I found the perfect outfit. I quickly used Mom's credit card to purchase a black, silk blouse and a multi-colored, skimpy skirt. I rushed into the shoe store and again used Mom's credit card to buy Johnny Woo, black, patent leather spike heels. Even though I was craving greasy French fries and a large soda, I remembered my promise to lose weight. Thus, I got in Mom's bulky sedan and sang with the radio all the way home.

On Friday afternoon, I got my hair cut and highlighted by Richard Von Thompson. His make-up artist showed me how to do my face. I used Mom's credit card to pay for new eye shadow, waterproof mascara, eyeliner, foundation, powder, lipstick, and Richard's services. The bill was almost $300, but it didn't matter. I was going out with Gorgeous Brown! Friday night, I laid in bed watching a cheesy, romantic, chick-flick . Oh, how I wanted some potato chips, onion dip, and a soda. However, I was on a diet, so I settled for an apple instead. At midnight, I texted Jen, "It's Saturday! I have a date in less than 19 hours with SGB."

"How can I forget?" she replied. "Want all details."

When I awoke the next morning to the delightful aroma of fried bacon, I realized that today was the day I had been waiting for--Saturday! I passed on Dad's culinary treat of bacon and eggs and slurped some cherry yogurt. I spent the rest of the day trying to finish Stupid Mr. Jansen's geometry homework and Bad Breath Kendall's history project, but I couldn't concentrate. My mind was focused on SGB's dark brown eyes, shaggy black hair, and awesome biceps.

After a low calorie dinner of broccoli and chicken, I began my preparation. I approached the bathroom scale. I reluctantly got on the scale and looked down. My determination had paid off; I had lost a half pound! I showered, washed and dried my Richard hair-do, and dressed. I carefully applied my make-up using the techniques I had learned yesterday. I styled my hair. I looked in the mirror; I looked fabulous.

Steven Gorgeous Brown arrived twenty minutes late. He was wearing his varsity football shirt that had a huge mustard stain in the middle of Property of CHS Athletic Department. His madras shorts were in tatters, and his 99 cent, rubber flip-flops were tinged with the green scum of lawn-mowing. It was obvious he had not shaved nor combed his hair in the last twenty-four hours. "Wow! You look great, " he said. "I didn't know you were so tall."

Tall? I was two inches taller than him in my spike heels! Gorgeous Brown was a bum, and I was gorgeous.

"Instead of going to the movies, Adam's having some friends over to watch the Tunas basketball game. It starts in fifteen, so we'd better get going."

"Should I change my clothes?" I stammered.

"Nah, you look great," he answered.

Against my better judgment, I went to Adam's party. I was one of three girls there who were dressed in faded, ripped jeans and Tuna, t-shirts. Everyone drank torpedo-sized sodas and crammed cheese curls down their throats. The fifteen boys stuffed themselves with pepperoni and onion pizzas and then engaged in a burping contest. The last two minutes of the game dragged on for twenty more. My feet hurt. Someone had accidently splashed strawberry soda on my skirt. Gorgeous Brown was doing one-hand, push-ups in front of the television. "When can I go home?" I wondered.

Finally, the Tunas won. Steven took me home and attempted to kiss me. He reeked of onions and garlic. He was not gorgeous, and I had no intention of kissing him. As I entered the house, my cell phone beeped. I viewed the text: "How was your date?"

"Jen, it sucked."

The Research Paper

If your teacher, college professor, or employer asks you to write a research paper and your writing skills suck the big wazoo, you need to follow our advice. While you may be tempted to pay someone else to write this paper or to steal a replica from the Internet, you suck! You are a dumb butt who paid good money for this book and are too stupid to realize that you are still stupid.

Buy, download, or borrow an English book that clearly delineates the research paper process. Our advice **merely summarizes** this task.

1. Gain an understanding of the assignment. Does the assignment ask you to discuss a process, to classify, to compare and/or to contrast, to persuade, to define, or to describe?

2. Pre-write until you can formulate one, clear, concise sentence, aka the **thesis statement.** This sentence is the road map or the force that controls the content of your paper. The following are examples:
- *The Indian Removal Act of 1830 was one of the most infamous occurrences in the history of humanity.*
- *The proposal of C. Deucethem and Howe is far superior to the proposals submitted by Jordan Landfill and Naughty Potty, LLC.*
- *The use of therapy dogs in hospitals improves both the physical and the psychological health of patients.*

3. Gather facts, statistics, and other information to support your thesis statement. Gone are the days of copying your essay from your parents' encyclopedia. You cannot write a quality research paper in ONE day. You must:

- Get off your fat, hind end, and go to the library.
- Use the Internet to search and retrieve information.
- Know the differences between good and bad, hard and soft, and primary and secondary evidence.

GOOD	BAD
Scholarly journals	Popular magazines
Refereed magazines	Tabloids
	On-line resources that can be edited

HARD	SOFT
Facts and statistics	Interpretations of data

PRIMARY	SECONDARY
Eyewitness accounts and/or photos	Interpretations of events
Original literary works	Book reviews
Speeches	Editorials
Historical documents	Biographies

(If in doubt about sources, email us at englishdoesntsuck.com)

- Scrutinize your sources to be sure they are credible and accurate. Always check the source (s) publication date.

With rapid technological and scientific discoveries, facts change. Uranus is a planet, not a body part.

4. Keep an accurate accounting of all sources, for you will need to document sources in the bibliography or "Works Cited" section of the paper. (If your teacher or professor dictates the citation style to be used, e.g. MLA, Chicago, or APA, use the Internet to help with formatting. We could explain each of these styles, but you only need to know which one you're **required** to use. After all, this style competition is educational bull s%#t.)

5. When you are ready to write your paper, arrange your thoughts chronologically, logically, or from least to most important.

6. Never copy word-for-word from a source unless you use quotation marks and appropriately credit the original author. *"There is no such thing as a brain fart; it is cranial flatulence."* (Creighton, 2008). If you choose to summarize or paraphrase a source, appropriately credit the author. *In her study of East Tennessee dialect, Creighton found no difference in the pronunciation of all and oil.* (2008).

 You Suck Uh-Oh!
Failure to give credit to the original author is plagiarism--a fancy word for stealing.

7. After writing your paper, seek assistance from the writing center, English teachers, and/or literate peers. Revise, revise, revise.

An example of a research paper, written in APA style follows on the next page. This is purely fictitious, so do not copy nor quote any of the information.

The Origin of the Toilet

Many people take their indoor, water-conserving, chocolate or red toilet for granted. They can only recall the days of the white, porcelain pot and are delighted that potties now come in custom colors with a variety of seats to satisfy any fantasy. However, research indicates that the evolution of the modern toilet spanned centuries.

In 202 B.C., the Han dynasty ruled China, and culture was elevated to new heights (Wright, 2004). After the second birthday of his son, I. Flingpoo, the Emperor held a summit. According to Han historian, Wright (2004), I. Fling suffered from an affliction that caused him to relieve himself in the Royal Gardens of Naaki and to attempt to toss his deposits over the Great Wall. In his address to the summit of inventors, the Emperor stated:

> The Empress and I are forever grateful that you are gathered here today. The troops of General Tse Tse Fli are complaining about the odors of the palace. Thus, we fear our dear son and heir to the throne, I. Fling, is in need of recreation. His current interest should be redirected to create a proper dumping ground for his talents. Expedience is a must. The first man to bring me a new device will live in luxury for the rest of his life. (p. 231)

Six months after the summit, several inventors responded. One had designed an apparatus resembling a modern-day sling shot; another offered a bead and string contraption for counting; a third presented a cumbersome, wood box. Research by Sunny and Char (2007) indicated that the Emperor was intrigued with the wooden box, faced with clear, glass screen. Its creator, X. Boxfu, demonstrated how a small, white ball could be batted back and forth across the screen. However, none of these devices proved effective. I. Fling became the Emperor in 170 B.C. and continued to decorate the neighborhood. (p. 167)

For the next 1,500 years, little attention was paid to bathrooming habits. Historian, Mia Angst (2004), noted, "People just liked doing it in the streets. They subscribed to the notion, 'When you've got to go, you've got to go,' regardless of the locale." (p. 41) As a result, disease was widespread, and some researchers estimate that over one million people died for lack of proper human waste disposal. (Charmain & Softones, 1995)

By1798, the death toll due to human pees and poops had climbed to four million. In America, people demanded that the government solve this pandemic. An unknown writer for the *Marblehead Mast* penned a scathing editorial:

> Hey, dudes. Wake up! We're a new country fraught with problems, and wallowing in feces shouldn't be one of them. It is urgent that Congress stop slinging doodoo and deal with it. If you fail to do it now, this will go on for another 300 years! By 2010, our heirs will be buried in piles of poop from which they will be unable to extricate themselves. Listen to distinguished Senator Sean O'Connor of Massachusetts, "Pahty should not take precedence over potty." (p. 3)

Despite the public outcry for intervention, the problem of proper human waste disposal continued. The Congress maintained it was a state problem; each state maintained it was a local problem. Thus, across America, municipalities, villages, and towns were faced with regulating "number 1" and "number 2". For example, Latimer, Alabama, City Council passed an ordinance that read in part: "Any person seen peeing on a tree or pooping in the grass will be subject to a $100 fine." (Sunny & Char, p. 69) Jefferson, Oregon, Village Trustees declared: "If you alleviate yourself in the backyard, wrap it up in newspaper, and throw it in the trash can. Failure to do so, may result in a fine." (Sunny & Char, p. 71) In Holbrook, Iowa, the voters approved this change to the town charter: "Human waste shall be dealt with accordingly: (a) dig a deep hole in the ground, do your business over the hole. When you are done, toss several shovels of dirt on top of it; (b) if you do not have a job, beat your girlfriend, nor have any good reason to stick around, drop yourself into a deep hole and get a friend to bury you." (Sunny & Char, p.82)

A number of distinguished women, led by schoolmarm, Rebeckah Johnson, convinced the mayor of Gopher Flats, West Virginia, that it was grossly inappropriate to see individuals squatting over earthen holes in their backyards. Johnson argued, "Young, impressionable minds should not witness such events while walking to and from school." In 1870, Mayor Boog Cates agreed and ordered that all holes had to be encased with a wooden structure. He signed unprecedented legislation that was known familiarly as the "Outhouse" law. (Fiddlefarts, 1912)

Then, in 1892, Ian and Ida Haddit left Scotland and came to the United States in search of a better life. While some historians noted that Haddit would have been satisfied to rent a New York City apartment, Ida convinced him to board a train and travel to Ashtabula, Ohio. (Fiddlefarts, p.17) In her diary, she wrote:

> Ian is dismayed that I insisted we move to Ashtabula, Indian words for "river of many fishes." However, I read the true account of the origin of the word, Ashtabula. Seems the Indian chief had an old wife named, Bulah. Then he took another gorgeous, young named Roxy. Throughout the remainder of the chief's life, he slept with his backside-to- Bulah. Sounds like my kind of place! (Haddit, p.5)

Once Haddit and Ida had settled into their environs on the Lake Erie shore, he became the verbal, punching bag of the Finnish and Italian immigrants with whom he worked. These dock workers, described as "hooligans" and "Satan's offspring", taunted Ian by denouncing Scotland as England's bastard child and by mispronouncing his name as Eye Am Going To.... (Zamboni, 1986) So with the permission of Ida, Ian anglicized his named to John. Most researchers posit that the Ian-to-John change led Haddit to reconsider his vocation. (Charmain and Softones, p.452)

For the next three years, Haddit designed and tinkered. He sawed, he hammered, he welded, he dug, and he tested. However, each of his creations failed. His meager savings account was nearly empty, forcing Ida to take in laundry and mending for wealthy, dock owners. "The cruelty of failure and of poverty compelled him to try one more time." He labored fourteen hours a day for two weeks, and on July 21, 1898, his apparatus was tested. Haddit sat down on the porcelain, emptied his bowels, wiped himself with a page from last year's catalog, reached above his head, and yanked the chain. (Charmain & Softones, p.560) According to a July 23 newspaper interview, Haddit, stated: "I was stunned! I was expecting to be covered again with spewing manure, but instead of going up, it went down! It went down. Down the pipe, down the pipe, and emptied into an underground tank. I did it!" When queried as to the name of his invention, Haddit replied, "John." (*Bula Blows,* p.6)

During the Victorian Era, Haddit's invention was renamed. Some historians have suggested that staid, proper, Victorian women found "John" to be offensive and preferred a more gentile term, "water closet." During the next century, Haddit's product underwent a number of changes. Cities built expansive sewer systems to accommodate the demand for waste removal. Eventually, rural outhouses became an artifact of the past. (Sunny & Char, p. 926)

The evolution of the modern toilet spanned centuries from the Han dynasty in 202 B.C. to a Lake Erie port in 1898. Though most historians credit John Haddit as the inventor, the dedication, determination, and perseverance of thousands made the toilet a reality. Without the combined efforts of these multitudes, the environmental sustainability of America would have been seriously compromised.

References

Angst, M. (2004). *Sewage in the streets: What a mess.* Boston: O' Leary and Sons.

Haddit Scores. [Interview with J. Haddit] (1898, July 23). *Bula Blows,* p. 6.

Charmain, U., & Softones, I. (1995). *The disposal of human waste.* New York: Randy Press.

Fiddlefarts, F. (1912). *Interesting facts of the 19th century.* Beech Springs: Mount Printing.

Haddit, I. (1892). *Personal diary entry.*

Government Must Act. (1799, August 12). *Marblehead Mast,* p. 3.

Sunny, S., & Char, E. (2007) *The history of bathrooming.* Dorset: Sandy University Press.

Wright, E. (2004). *Contributions of the han dynasty to modern society.* Orwell: Rock Creek Publishing.

Zamboni, Z. (1986) *A question of tolerance: The shipping industry nightmares.* Harbor: Lake College for Erie Women Press.

Revising Strategies

We are well aware that this picture is crude and disgusting, but we must have your full attention as we near the end of the writing section.

Ernest Hemingway once said, "The first draft of anything is s@#$." If you forget to revise, your writing will not only suck, it will be crap! Great writing is the result of rewriting, revising, and massaging--a foreign concept in an instant-messaging world. Hello, you are not perfect, nor is Bitsy Blondell. Remember this awful paragraph? Bitsy needs to revise it.

Dogs and Me

by Bitsy Blondell

    Dogs are great companions for single girls. How do I know that? My life sucks! If I had a dog, I'd have companionship. Dogs are friends. My dog would love me. Even though I forget my homework and hate chemistry formulas. My dog would replace my friends. My friends party too much and never text unless they need a ride. Not to mention all those dumb boys that ask me out once and never call again!! If I had a dog, I would be sooo happy. Just a little dog. I wouldn't even mind cleaning up pee on the carpet. Dogs are single girls' best friends. If I can't get a dog, I'll get a kitten.

1. Vary sentences. Adults don't talk baby talk. When adults write baby talk sentences, their writing sucks! Look at Bitsy's sentences.

- Dogs are friends.
- My dog would love me.

The use of more complex and longer sentences indicates not only adulthood, but also intelligence and sophistication. Bitsy's sentences might be rewritten as:

- Regardless of their size, dogs are loyal and protective of their owner.
- **Dogs are better than children: dogs don't talk back, beg for a ride to the mall, nor borrow money for a night at the movies. *(AT)**

2. Use specific words, such as lively adjectives, vivid verbs, and words that relate to the five senses. An on-line or hard copy Thesaurus can help identify descriptive words.

- I want a dog. (Boring)
- I want a registered, black, miniature poodle puppy. (Specific)
- Bitsy lives in an apartment. (Boring)
- Bitsy's gloomy, one-bedroom, apartment on the corner of Elm and Ash had deteriorated into a ruin of cracked

windows, peeling paint, and termite-infested lumber. (Specific)
- Bitsy said she'd be back later. (Instead of "said, " spoke, whispered, mumbled, cried, yelled, sobbed, screamed are vivid verbs)
- The annoying, intercom buzzer was whirring in Bitsy's ear. (Sense of Hearing)
- Bitsy's room reeked of spoiled yogurt, gardenia perfume, and dog pee. (Sense of Smell)

3. Use transitions to help the reader follow the writer's thoughts. Transitions are words and phrases that show logical connections and relationships between ideas. Transitions send signals to the reader about time, place, examples, conclusions, comparisons and contrasts. Below are given some common transitions:

	next	since	beyond	such as
second (ly)	soon	in retrospect	to the left	for example
third (ly)	until	in summary	above	specifically
last (ly)	similarly	in conclusion	to the right	in spite of
finally	in contrast	thus	opposite	nevertheless
in conclusion	on one hand	therefore	because	however

after (wards)	on the other hand	as mentioned earlier	as previously stated	on the contrary
again	although	below	in fact	in short

4. **Organize ideas** to convince the reader that writer is knowledgeable. Bitsy's thoughts are so scattered and hard to follow. She attempts to convince us she wants a dog, and then out of NOWHERE says she'll settle for a kitten! Bitsy is crazy. What sane person would want to cope with a litter box, fur balls, and claws?

5. **Use technology,** such as "spell check" or "grammar check," available in most word processing programs. Bitsy forgot to do so.

- Misspelled *"so"*
- Overused the exclamation mark
- Wrote sentence fragments: *Even though I forget me homework and hate chemistry formulas. Not to mention all those dumb boys that ask me out once and never call again!!*

6. **Read** your writing aloud. Does it make sense? Does it wander aimlessly? Is your precise opinion clear? Have **at least** one other person read it. Another pair of eyes usually can spot errors and omissions. Finally, try reading your paper backwards. If it is well-organized, it should be just as clear as when you read it forward.

Since we royally trashed Bitsy's paragraph, she asked for the opportunity to rewrite it. Behold her next attempt:

Dogs and Me

by Bitsy Blondell

Dogs are great companions for single women. I came to understand that at the end of my sophomore year. I had managed to squeak by with a "C-" in chemistry but had excruciating headaches from memorizing stupid formulas. My so-called friends took off for a week in San Diego; they didn't ask me to go. They had enough cars and drivers. My lab partner, Mark, never called to confirm his promise of a date to the baseball game. Summer was here; life sucked. Then, I decided to get a dog to add some vitality to my boring life as a friendless waif and part-time waitress at Juang's Pizzeria. After visiting several animal shelters without success, old, mean Juang said his registered, miniature black poodle had been diddled by some mangy stray and was due to have pups any day. If I could wait six weeks, Juang would give me one of his mutts. Seven weeks later, I was holding an adorable black and brown stoodle (half stray; half poodle), whom I named Sadie. Sadie saved my summer. As the start of my junior approaches, I am not worried about having friends or dates. I have Sadie; she makes me walk through Central Park and window shop along Fifth Avenue. She snuggles against me as we watch our previously, recorded soap operas, and she sleeps at my head every night. Sadie and I talk about everything; she seems to sense when I need a lick or a cuddle. Perhaps, she will help me pass trigonometry this year. Sadie has brought security and joy to my life as a junior girl who just may take Sadie to the prom.

"Paparazzi and Tabloids...enough said."

Things that are SICK and WRONG

Sick and Wrong: Phonics Gone Awry

Momma was in the kitchen preparing macaroni and cheese. Six-year-old Kayla was reading a book to her baby brother. "Look at the picture, Tommy. It's a frickin' flower. It's a frickin' violet."

Momma knocked over the box of macaroni, the cheesy powder dusted the counter. She rushed into the playroom and demanded, "Kayla! What did you say?"

"Look, Momma."

African Violet

Things That Are Just Sick and Wrong

Poor speech and stupid spelling make us crazy! We do not give a horse's hind end about your geographic locale, nor do we care that you heard it or saw it in the media. If you make these mistakes, you're ignorant, and you suck.

- irregardless (NOT a word; regardless is a word.)
- ain't or tain't (Correct form: am not, is not, are not)
- Where are you at? (Correct form: Where are you?)
- I'm fixin' to go to the library. (Really? What are you going to get fixed?)
- She can't hardly wait to cram her body into spandex and go to the gym. (Correct form: She can't wait to cram her body into spandex and go to the gym.)
- If flying be safe, why do I have to go to the airport terminal? (Correct form: If flying is safe, why do I have to go to the airport terminal?)
- yens and yous (Correct form: you. We don't care if you're from Pittsburgh!)
- ain't got no (Correct form: do not have)
- These ones are mine. (Correct form: These are mine. These nail files are mine.)
- Your dog is pretty ugly. (Uh-oh, and to think you spent all that money on a mutt.)
- Betcha Noah wished he had kilt them two mosquitoes. (Correct form: I bet Noah wished that he had killed those two mosquitoes.)
- dat (Correct form: that. Again, we don't care if you play professional sports.)

On the internet and in English texts, there are lists of commonly misspelled words. However, these are our favorites that have left us convulsed in laughter because we know these writers are dorkuses!

- Youthinasia is a serious problem. (We agree overpopulation is a problem in the Orient, but you meant to write euthanasia.)
- The valleyvictorian strutted across the stage and high-fived her principal. (Was the writer describing a character from a Dickens' novel? No, the valedictorian.)
- youraneight. (How many times do I have to take the random drug test until score a 10? Urinate is the correct spelling.

When in doubt as to how spell a word correctly, look in the dictionary, get the computer to spell it, or choose other words that have similar meaning. If you can't spell *pneumonia*, use dreadfully-bad chest cold. If you can't spell *onomatopoeia*, use the buzzword.

"You will survive my teenaged angst."

Parent Advice

Parent Advice

The following is a true story. George, a dentist, graduated thirty years ago from a prestigious eastern university. While he enjoys a very lucrative career as a dentist, last year he was elected president of the state dental society. His position required he write a monthly article in the society's newsletter. "Sue, I have hated English since grade school. It does suck! I am a successful dentist, but I cannot put words on paper. I have avoided writing my entire, professional career, and by accepting this presidency, I must write something coherent and intelligent. Unfortunately, I can't go on the web, like my teenage son does for his term paper assignments, and steal an article about the lack of dental hygiene in Mesa, Arkansas."

Even if your children are destined to be speech therapists or nuclear physicists, writing is an important skill to master. While many will gnash their braces and throw diva tantrums, it can be done without much angst and anxiety. Now imagine this scenario: your child has been assigned to write a paper on any topic he/she chooses. "I can't think of anything. I don't know where to start," your child whines. It is your job to guide him/her through the writing process steps.

1. Prewriting or finding a manageable topic that can be presented in *one*, logical sentence.

- Ask your child questions. What was the best birthday present you ever got? What was the scariest thing that ever happened to you? What will happen if you fail algebra? How to you make a paper airplane? Describe your date to the prom? Why do you want to be an accountant? How do the Chinese celebrate New Year? What was the significance of Jonas Salk's contribution to modern medicine?

- When your child expresses interest in an idea, doodle it.

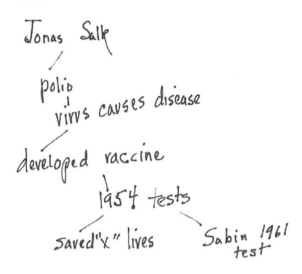

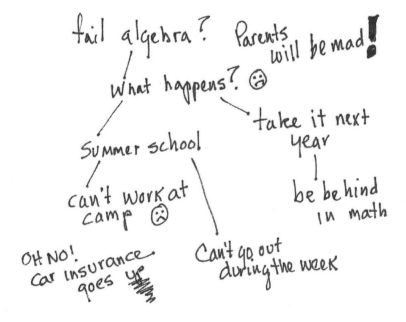

- Once the doodling is completed, have your child draft one sentence about the topic. For example, *Jonas Salk made a significant contribution to modern medicine when he discovered a polio vaccine*, or *If I fail algebra, I will face several consequences.*
- This sentence is known as the **topic sentence** in paragraphs or the **thesis statement** in longer papers, such as essays or research work. The sentence controls the content of the paper and serves as a road map for both the writer and the reader.

 You Suck Uh-Oh!

- Many young writers have great difficulty limiting the topic to one that is manageable. Their topics are **too broad**, as: how I spent my summer vacation, students in high school have many problems, or the causes and effects of global warming on the world. Often their topics are **shallow**, as: I like skiing because it is fun, I have a brother named Brian, or green is my favorite color. In these cases, a meaningful paper can rarely be produced. (A detailed list of suggested topics for each essay style follows.)
- Using either the paragraph format or essay format form found in the appendix, have your child fill in the blanks as illustrated:

Topic sentence: Jonas Salk made a significant contribution to modern medicine....

Supporting Evidence 1: Numbers of people stricken with polio throughout history

Details: From 1400 BC to Franklin D. Roosevelt, increased number of afflicted, facts

Supporting Evidence 2: Link between virus and disease

Details: Developed vaccine based on research findings, field tested 1954, school kids

Supporting Evidence 3: Sabin develops oral vaccine from Salk formula

Details: Oral vaccine 1961, distributed to school kids, funded

Closing: Without the efforts of Salk, thousands of children would have been crippled or would have died from polio.

Topic sentence: If I fail algebra, I will face serious consequences.

Details: Bummer. Get up early, study in afternoon, no time for fun

Supporting Evidence 2: Can't go out during the week

Details: Miss my friends, won't go to baseball games, won't go to swim parties

Supporting Evidence 3: Can't work at the Y Camp

Details: Hours don't coincide, won't be able to pay car insurance.

Closing: If I fail algebra, my life will be awful this summer.

2. Writing

- Send your child off to write. ***Do not write the paper for him/her.***

3. Revising

- Revising is *most important.* In our world of instant messaging, disasters can occur when the "send" key is pressed. Recently, the stock market was sent into an unprecedented slide, solely due to a typographical error in an instant message.
- Revising takes time but will greatly benefit writing. A revising checklist follows:

Revising Strategies for the Writer

- Read your paper aloud. Does it make sense?
- Read your paper from backward to forward. Does it make sense?
- If you typed it on the computer, run spell check.

Revising Strategies for the Parent Proofreader

- If the paper is handwritten, is it legible?
- Does the paper make sense?
- Is it free of spelling errors, smiley faces, hearts, and instant messaging abbreviations, such as LOL, BFF, and BTW? Remember spell check will not identify errors for the misuse of correctly spelled words, for example, then for than or hole for whole.

- Is there an overuse of the same word? He said, then I said, then he said, and I said. Use a thesaurus to find more vivid verbs for said, such as asked, replied, cried, whispered, screamed, shouted, etc.
- Is there a conclusion to the paper? It should not read as a "to be continued" television soap opera.
- In your estimation, does the paper represent your child's best effort?

Suggested Topics by Essay Style

Narration:

1. If I could relive a memory, I
2. If I could pick a super power, I
3. If I could do one thing over again, I
4. Working as a baby sitter was the most frustrating job I ever had.
5. When I was twelve years old, the only thing I could think about was learning to drive a car.
6. The best thing that ever happened to me was
7. The worst thing that ever happened to me was
8. On the school bus this morning, the funniest thing occurred
9. After I was chosen for the football team, my nightmare began
10. I really disappointed my family, when I got caught
11. I was so proud of myself when I
12. I never cried so hard as the night that
13. I was terrified when
14. I will never forget the day that

Persuasive:

1. Write a letter your parents persuading them that you need…

2. Imagine Dunkin Donuts® is having a contest for a new donut recipe/design. Describe your design and flavor, then write a letter to the CEO persuading him that he should choose yours.
3. Nature conservancy-land being re-allocated for housing development. Write a letter to editor in support of the NC.
4. Letter to a company trying to convince it how it can go green.
5. Write a letter to someone trying to convince him/her that he/she should go out with you.
6. Schools place too much emphasis on competition.
7. High school proms should be abolished.
8. Christmas is too commercialized.
9. Students should be allowed to have cell phones at school.
10. [fill-in-the-blank] should be legalized.

Compare/Contrast

1. Dogs are better than cats.
2. Cats are better than dogs.
3. Flying is more convenient than driving.
4. High school is better than middle school.
5. Going to school is easier than working.
6. Of the two candidates for class president, John Black is superior to Ryan Brown.
7. *Grinding in LA* is a much better movie than its sequel, *Grinding in DC*.
8. Before I moved to California, after I moved to California
9. Before I met Jake, after I met Jake
10. Writing an essay is as painful as going to the dentist.
11. Ice hockey is similar to roller-blade hockey.
12. My school is like a candy store.
13. What are the differences between McDoody's fast food restaurant menus in Tokyo and Los Angeles?

Cause and Effect

1. Why I quit playing the piano/football/video games
2. Why I like to...
3. Why I dislike...
4. Why I overslept/ why I didn't do my homework/ why I didn't...
5. What will happen if I quit playing piano/football/ video games
6. When my best friend was hospitalized, I....
7. When I decided to get a part-time job, I faced several consequences.
8. Transferring to a new school changed my life in positive ways.
9. My grandfather changed my life when he...
10. There are three major reasons why Mark Twain wrote *The Adventures of Huckleberry Finn*.
11. Following the discovery of [fill-in-the-blank], the results were astounding.

Process

1. How to make a paper airplane, peanut butter and jelly sandwich, or a web site.
2. How to entertain oneself when grounded for an entire weekend.
3. How to look smart when you are just bluffing.
4. How to shop for designer clothes on a tiny allowance.
5. How to bathe a hamster. (Why would anyone in his/her right mind want to do that?)
6. How I came to learn that I should never lie to my girlfriend/boyfriend.
7. How I was taught the importance of community service.
8. How were the bodies of Egyptian kings mummified?

9. How does a specific culture/religion/ country celebrate...?
10. How did Ben Franklin discover electricity?

Description

1. I could tell when I walked into his/her bedroom that a/an... lived there. Basketball player, astronomy geek, movie worshipper, dirt bag, rock star, dog lover, idol fan, artist, musician, dentist, nurse, nerd, etc.
2. Describe your grandparents' cabin, your favorite hideout, an amazing cheeseburger, the best pizza, or an organism
3. Describe your dream vacation, dream date, or dream career
4. Describe drivers: teenagers, gangstas, snowbirds, elderly
5. What does anger/love/hate/humor look like? Feel like? Smell like? Taste like? Hear like?

Expository/Research

1. The history of Rock and Roll music
2. The origin of the cell phone/computer/public sanitation
3. The First Amendment to the Constitution and student rights to free speech
4. The five greatest inventions in the world
5. The Puritan influence of author, Herman Smellville, in his best-selling novel, *Willy Dud.*
6. Loneliness and alienation are the themes of three poems by Danger Stranger.
7. Emily Sickinson's song, *I Hate Cats,* was a tribute to her mentor, I. Shih-tzu.
8. The psychology of advertising on teenaged consumers
9. Columbus did not discover America and other myths.
10. A field study of the effects of long-term consumption of popsicles on the nutrient health of gerbils.

"The use of recording devices is strictly prohibited during practice sessions."

Practice

Practice: The Sentence

The following may be complete sentences, fragments, or run-ons. Indicate C for complete, F for fragment, RO for run-on.

1.____When Bruce was in kindergarten.

2.____He had the bad habit of leaving his pajamas on the floor when he'd finished dressing.

3.____His mom nagged him endlessly to pick them up but he refused to do so.

4.____Worrying about how to break this habit.

5.____Mom told Bruce that she would charge him two cents for each time she picked up his pajamas.

6.____Bruce reached in his pocket he took out a dime.

7.____"Pick them up for the rest of the week."

Answers

1. F

2. C

3. RO

4. F

5. C

6. RO

7. C

When Bruce was in kindergarten, he had the bad habit of leaving his pajamas on the floor when he'd finished dressing. His mom nagged him endlessly to pick them up, but he refused to do so. Worrying about how to break this habit, Mom told Bruce that she would charge him two cents for each time she picked up his pajamas. Bruce reached in his pocket; he took out a dime. "Pick them up for the rest of the week."

Punctuation Practice Sentences

1. On April 18 1775 Paul Revere rode his horse through the streets shouting The British are coming
2. Revere could have saved a great deal of time if he would have texted the patriots this message BTW Brits r here
3. After it stopped raining I went to the library the mall and the ice cream store
4. The following should be avoided rattlesnakes scorpions and Black Widow spiders
5. Jasons sister in law is in medical school in Greenville Indiana
6. Jen and her brother Marcus spent a week in San Diego at the beach they got raging sunburns
7. Its too bad that more people dont adopt dogs from the animal shelters
8. My six year old cousin announced that he was running away from home he packed his lunch box and sat at the end of the driveway for less than twenty minutes
9. Youre not going out of the house wearing those filthy jeans declared Aunt Florence
10. Wow What happened to your hair
11. Since his so called friend Jose didnt pick him up after school he walked home
12. One can hardly imagine a world without computers, for they are much more convenient than encyclopedias.

Answers follow on the next page

1. On April 18, 1775, Paul Revere rode his horse through the streets shouting, "The British are coming!"
2. Revere could have saved a great deal of time if he would have texted the patriots this message: BTW Brits r here!
3. After it stopped raining, I went to the library, the mall, and the ice cream store.
4. The following should be avoided: rattlesnakes, scorpions, and Black Widow spiders.
5. Jason's sister-in-law is in medical school in Greenville, Indiana.
6. Jen and her brother, Marcus, spent a week in San Diego at the beach; they got raging sunburns.
7. It's too bad that more people don't adopt dogs from the animal shelters.
8. My six-year-old cousin announced that he was running away from home; he packed his lunch box and sat at the end of the driveway for less than twenty minutes.
9. "You're not going out of the house wearing those filthy jeans," declared Aunt Florence.
10. Wow! What happened to your hair?
11. Since his so-called friend, Jose, didn't pick him up after school, he walked home.
12. Correct

Practice Agreement: Pronouns

If necessary, correct the following sentences to make pronouns agree in number or person with the nouns to which they refer.

1. The teenager is a curious sort; he or she/ they sleeps all day and roams all night.
2. The dog strolled onto the neighbor's property and doo-dooed in her/their backyard.
3. Many fast food restaurants require its/their employees to submit to random drug testing.
4. If everyone is going to the beach for spring break, he or she/ they needs to bring sunscreen.
5. Some members of the class are not going to pass the test; he or she/they will need to do an extra-credit project.
6. **Dogs are better than children; they/dogs don't whine, beg for a ride to the mall, or refuse to shop at a store that ends in Mart. *(AT)**

Answers

1. he or she
2. her
3. their
4. he or she
5. they
6. dogs

Practice Agreement

Choose the correct verb form:

1. Does/Do everyone on the cheer squad want to ride in the van, or does/do some of you want to drive yourselves?
2. The grove of aspen trees is/are alive with killer bees.
3. One hundred years has/have gone by since acne was discovered, yet no cures has/have been found.
4. The rock band, GeekStars, performs/perform nightly at the West Side Cafe.
5. Neither Rob nor Cindy is/are going to the firework show after the football game.
6. Why has/have no one discovered a device that allows people to text and drive at the same time?
7. Gossip about Hollywood stars sells/sell teeny bopper magazines.
8. Early dismissal days, Monday holidays, and teacher workdays is/are the best thing about school.
9. **A computer, a cell phone, and a full tank of gas makes/make sixteen-year olds happy. *(AT)**
10. He don't/doesn't do his homework because it don't/doesn't get graded by the teacher.

Answers

1. Does/do
2. Is
3. have/have
4. performs
5. is
6. has
7. sells
8. are
9. make
10. doesn't/doesn't

Practice: Split Infinitives, Dangling Participles, Misplaced Modifiers, and Faulty Parallelism

The following are either correct as written or in need of revision.

1. My grandfather came to live with us at the age of six.
2. While driving home from the baseball game, two fans were brawling in the middle of the street.
3. Except when roasted, I don't like peppers.
4. The skateboard was twenty-five inches long and seven inches in width.
5. I wanted to quickly finish my homework, so I could watch my favorite, afternoon soap opera.
6. Ashley likes English, Spanish, and playing tennis on the varsity team.
7. After playing video games all morning, the bed still was not made.
8. The child went careening down the driveway just as we arrived on a tricycle.
9. Andre sings, dances, and has a starring role in *Revenge of the Pimple Squeezer.*
10. Mrs. Higginbottom loves to really pile on the homework on Fridays.

Answers

1. When I was six-years-old, my grandfather came to live with us.

2. While driving home from the baseball game, I saw two fans brawling in the middle of the street.

3. I don't like peppers unless they're roasted.

4. The skateboard was twenty-five inches long and seven inches wide.

5. I wanted to finish my homework quickly, so I could watch my favorite, afternoon soap opera.

6. Ashley likes English, Spanish, and varsity tennis.

7. The bed was still not made because I had played video games all morning.

8. Just as we arrived, the child went careening down the driveway on a tricycle.

9. Andre sings, dances, and stars in *Revenge of the Pimple Squeezer*.

10. Mrs. Higginbottom really loves to pile on the homework on Fridays.

Practice: Goof Ball Spelling

Choose the correct word.

1. In *To Kill a Mockingbird,* the character development of Atticus Finch was a better than/then the character development of Scout. Scout was to/too unbelievable.
2. We wanted to go to strings' concert, but are/our friends find violin music boring.
3. The affects/effects of texting 'til 2:00 AM greatly affected/effected my performance on the math placement test.
4. According to some, there/their/they're many ways be successful; however, there/their/they're dreamers.
5. Who's/whose stinky socks are on the floor? The hole/whole pile needs to be put in the washer.
6. The principal/principle at our school has no idea as to whether/weather or not students are seeking advice/advise about scholarships.
7. Maria was accepted/excepted into the honor society, but she missed the induction/deduction ceremony because she lost her cell phone. (She also said she had nothing to wear/where.)
8. Its/It's funny to/two watch a reality TV show. Its/It's plot is so stupid, and its/it's theme sucks.
9. Denice past/passed her eye exam because she had studied the night before.
10. Even though I hit the brakes/breaks on my scooter, I managed to brake/break my wrist when I fell.

Answers

1. than, too

2. our

3. effects, effected

4. there, they're

5. Whose , whole

6. principal, whether

7. accepted, induction, wear

8. It's, Its, its

9. passed

10. brakes, break

Practice: Sins 6 and 7

In the passed, my family loved me, but I am about to be kicked out of the house due to the fact that I'd rather do nothing then do something. Mom has excused me of using her house as a hotel, restaurant, and a laundry. There can be no doubt that on occasion I've laid on the sofa, eaten a hole box of cookies, and tracked to much mud on the bathroom rug. I want to be well, butt sometimes I can't. Today, thorough, my mom freaked when the principle called and said I'd missed training class again. She was greatly effected by that call and yelled. You never know weather or not she'll forgive me or get rid of me!!!!!

Correct Edit

In the **past,** my family loved me, but I am about to be kicked out of the house because I **would** rather do nothing **than** something. Mom has **accused** me of using her house as a hotel, restaurant, and laundry. On occasion I **have lain** on the sofa, eaten a **whole** box of cookies, and tracked **too** much mud in the bathroom rug. I want to be **good, but** sometimes I **cannot.** Today **though,** my mom freaked when the **principal** called and said I **had** missed training class again. She was greatly **affected** by that call and yelled. **I do not know whether** or not she **will forgive** me or get rid of me!

(The author's picture follows on the next page.)

SORRY

Acknowledgements

A number of dedicated people were instrumental in guiding us through this endeavor. We appreciate the generosity of Randy Bronner, our banking advisor, and Greg Podd, our accounting guru. We are grateful for the work of our artists, Kolby McLean and Will Zandler, for bringing our words to illustration. Further, we thank Principal Arnholdt for his mentoring and our favorite Happy Hour establishment, Z Tejas, for quenching our thirst.

"Consider this as an encore."

Appendix

Paragraph Format

Topic
Sentence:_____

Supporting Evidence 1:
_____
_____

Details:
_____
_____

Supporting Evidence 2:
_____
_____

Details:
_____
_____

Supporting Evidence 3:
_____
_____

Details:
_____
_____

Closing:_____

Essay Format

Introduction and Thesis Statement:

_____

Body Paragraph 1

Topic Sentence:

_____
_____

Supporting Evidence:

_____
_____

Details:

_____

Body Paragraph 2

Topic Sentence:

_____
_____

Supporting Evidence:

_____
_____

Details:

_____

Body Paragraph 3:

Topic Sentence:

_____

_____

Supporting Evidence:

_____

_____

Details:

_____

Conclusion and restatement of thesis:

_____

_____

"My roadies can find everything, even my contact lens."

Index

Index

Absolute truth, xv - xvi
Adjective, 5 - 6
Adverb, 6
Apostrophe, 17 - 20
    practice, 125
Appendix, 137
Argumentation paper, 66 - 67
    example, 68 - 69
Bad and badly, 38
Bring and take, 37
Business communications, 53 - 56
    email, 53 - 54
    letter, 55 - 56
Cause/Effect paper, 73 - 74
    example, 75 - 77
Colon, 20 - 21
Comma, 14 - 17
    practice, 125
Compare/Contrast paper, 70 - 71
    example, 72
Confusing words list, 39 - 44
    practice, 131 - 132
Conjunction, 7 - 8
Contractions, 18 - 20
    in formal writing, 36
Dangling participle, 33
    practice, 129 - 130
Deadwood, 35
Description paper, 84 - 85
    example, 86 - 88
Diarrhea sentence, 28 - 29
    practice, 129
Email, 53 - 54
Essay, 52 - 58
    example, 58 - 59
    format, 140

styles, 60 - 61
Exclamation point, 13
   practice, 125
Faulty parallelism, 34 - 35
   practice, 133 - 134
Good and well, 38
Hyphen, 22 - 23
   practice, 125
Interjection, 8 -9
Lay and lie, 37
Loose and lose, 37
Misplaced modifier, 33 - 34
   practice, 129 - 130
Narrative paper, 62 - 63
   example, 64 - 65
Noun, 3
Paragraph, 51 – 52, 139
Parent Advice, 111 - 117
Period, 13
   practice, 125
Persuasion paper, see Argumentation, 67
Practices, 123 - 134
Preposition, 6 - 7
Prewriting, 47 – 48, 111 - 112
Process paper, 78 - 79
   example, 80 - 83
Pronoun, 3 - 4
   antecedent, 30 - 31
   practice, 127
Question mark, 13 - 14
Quotation marks, 21 - 22
   practice, 125
Research paper, 89 - 91
   example, 92 - 96
Revising strategies, 98 – 102, 115 - 116
Semicolon, 21
Sentence, 5, 27
   fragment, 28

    practice, 123
Split infinitive, 32
    practice, 129 – 130
Subject-verb agreement, 29
    practice, 128
Suggested Topics by Essay Style, 116 - 119
Than and then, 37
There in formal writing, 36
There, their, they're confusion, 20
Time zone agreement, 31 - 32
Topic sentence, 47, 51, 57 – 58, 113 - 114
Transitions, 100 - 101
Verb, 4
Whose and who's confusion, 20
Writing, 97
You in formal writing, 36
Your and you're confusion, 20

Phleby, don't jump. It's a MOSH PIT! Oh, no....

Made in the USA
Charleston, SC
11 November 2010